Vocabulary: The Personal Dictionary

Simbo Nuga

Available from Amazon.com and other retailers, or e-mail orders@liberty-stowe.com.
Printed by CreateSpace, an Amazon.com company
Copyright © 2017 Simbo Nuga
ISBN: 978-0-9928964-7-8
British Library Cataloguing in Publication Data
A catalogue record for this title is available from the British Library.

All rights reserved. No part of this publication may be reproduced, stored in a retrieval system, or transmitted in any form or by any means, electronic, mechanical, photocopying, recording, scanning, or otherwise, without the prior permission of the author or except in accordance with the provisions of the Copyright, Design and Patents Act 1988.
Limit of Liability/Disclaimer of Warranty: The publisher and the author make no representation or warranties with respect to the accuracy or completeness of the contents of this work and specifically disclaim all warranties, including without limitation warranties of fitness for a particular purpose. No warranty may be created or extended by sales or promotional materials. The advice and strategies contained herein may not be suitable for every situation. This work is sold with the understanding that the publisher is not engaged in rendering medical, legal or other professional advice or service. If professional assistance is required, the services of a competent professional person should be sought. Neither the publisher nor the author shall be liable for damages arising henceforth. The fact than an individual or organisation is referred to in this work as a citation and/or potential source of further information does not mean that the author or the publisher endorses the information the individual, organisation, or website may provide or recommendations they/it may make. Further, readers should be aware that Internet websites listed in this work may have changed or disappeared between when this work was written and when it is read.

DEDICATION

With gratitude to

You

This personal dictionary belongs to:

_____

Table of Contents

DEDICATION III
TABLE OF CONTENTS IV
ACKNOWLEDGEMENT VII
PREFACE 1
PART 1 VOCABULARY 3
    INTRODUCTION 4
    I. ALPHABETICAL LIST OF USEFUL WORDS 6
    II. MNEMONICS 56
    iii. List of Alliterations 67
    IV. LIST OF OXYMORA 69
PART 2 GENERAL KNOWLEDGE QUESTIONS 71
    I. INTRODUCTION 72
    II. GENERAL KNOWLEDGE QUESTIONS 72
    III. ANSWERS TO GENERAL KNOWLEDGE QUESTIONS 96
PART 3 VOCABULARY WORKSHEETS 100
    I. INTRODUCTION 101
    II. NAMES OF ANIMALS 102
    III. ARCHITECTURE 102
    IV. ART 104
    V. TYPES OF CLOTHING 105
    VI. COOKERY 106
    VII. ELECTRICAL TERMS 107
    VIII. EVERYDAY THINGS 108
    IX. EXTERNAL PARTS OF THE HUMAN BODY 109
    X. FINANCIAL TERMS 110
    XI. NAMES OF FRUITS 111
    XII. TYPES OF GAMES AND SPORTS 112
    XIII. GEOGRAPHY 113
    XIV. HISTORY 114
    XV. THINGS FOUND IN A HOUSE 115
    XVI. LEGAL TERMS 116
    XVII. LITERARY TERMS 117

XVIII. MATHEMATICS	118
XIX. MEDICAL TERMS	119
XX. PARTS OF AN ANIMAL	120
XXI. PARTS OF A BIRD	121
XXII. TERMS USED FOR PEOPLE (FAMILY AND FRIENDS)	122
XXIII. PLACES	123
XXIV. PROFESSIONS	124
XXV. RELIGIONS OF THE WORLD	125
XXVI. SCHOOL (PEOPLE AND THINGS)	126
XXVII. SCIENCE	127
XXVIII. SEWING	128
XXIX. NAMES OF VEGETABLES	129

PART 4 CONFUSABLE WORDS 130

INTRODUCTION	131
TABLE 1 CONFUSABLE WORDS	146
TABLE 2 HOMOGRAPHS	149
TABLE 3 HOMONYMS	151
TABLE 4 HOMOPHONES	151

PART 5 REFERENCE MATERIALS 155

INTRODUCTION	156
A. DAYS OF THE WEEK	156
B. NAMES OF MONTHS AND NUMBER OF DAYS	156
C. EXPRESSIONS OF TIME	157
D. NAMES OF SEASONS AROUND THE WORLD	157
E. COLOURS	157
F. THINGS WE CANNOT COUNT	158
G. ANIMALS: PARENT, YOUNG, MALE AND FEMALE	159
H. COUNTRIES, CITIZENS CAPITALS, CURRENCIES AND LANGUAGES	163
I. SPELLING NUMBERS CORRECTLY	169
J. ROMAN NUMERALS	170
K. PREFIXES	171
L. SUFFIXES	174

PART 6 USEFUL RESOURCES 175

LIST OF RESOURCES	176

- Appendix 1 Words that I have learnt 177
- Appendix 2 Personal Learning Objective Sheet 177
- Appendix 3 Study Plan 179
- Appendix 4 reading record 181
- Appendix 5 Spelling Practice Sheet 181
- Appendix 6 Extra Vocabulary Sheet 182
- Appendix 7 Word Usage Practice Sheet 183
- Appendix 8 Confusable words practice sheet 184
- Appendix 9 Book Review 185
- Appendix 10A Write Your Own List Of Words 185
- Appendix 10B Write Your Own List Of Word s 187
- Appendix 11 Mnemonic Form 188

REFERENCES **188**

USEFUL WEBSITES **190**

Notes 194

ACKNOWLEDGEMENTS

I would like to thank my husband and children for their sacrifice and support during the compilation of this book. My sincere appreciation goes to my family and friends for being a source of encouragement.

Simbo Nuga

Preface

"Words are, of course, the most powerful drug used by mankind."
— *Rudyard Kipling*

In today's global village and reliance on technology, competition for college places and jobs continues to increase. The ability to communicate effectively improves an individual's ability to succeed in education, in career and in life.

This book is a practical resource that is useful for building and improving your vocabulary. It has six parts: vocabulary, general knowledge questions, word categories, confusable words, reference materials and useful resources.

Part 1 has a step-by-step guide to learning and remembering new words. It presents alphabetical lists of words and examples of how to use mnemonic devices. The words of each alphabet include separate lists of three and four letter words followed by a final list with more letters. These words include important and more advanced English words. Appendix 1, *Words That I Have Learnt,* is a handy summary sheet to record your progress.

Part 2 has sets of general knowledge questions, presented alphabetically. These have been included because general knowledge questions are included in selection processes and the possession of such useful information contributes to a candidate's success. The answers are also provided.

Part 3 provides ample worksheets about various aspects of everyday life. Each worksheet provides an alphabetical list of useful words related to a particular subject. There are blank spaces for more words to be added. Appendices 10A and 10B are useful templates for writing new categories of words.

Part 4 provides clarity on words that are often misspelt and misused. It has explanations and examples of confusable words, homographs, homonyms and homophones. There is also a comprehensive exercise to be completed.

Part 5 has some valuable reference materials and includes information on the days of the week, months of the year, seasons, colours, spelling of numbers, a list of the names of animals, expressions of time, a list of countries, the names of their respective capital cities, citizens, currencies and languages, roman numerals and a list of prefixes and suffixes.

Part 6 has helpful resources to enable you practise the spelling of new words, write sentences, set personal learning goals, plan study times, write book reviews and new categories of words.

PART 1

Vocabulary

One forgets words as one forgets names.
One's vocabulary needs constant fertilizing or it will die.
- Evelyn Waugh

Introduction

In this part of the book, words are presented alphabetically and at the beginning of each list is the relevant phonetic alphabet. Phonetic alphabets or spelling alphabets are often used to verbally communicate the exact spelling and pronunciation of a word. Each letter has three sets of words and the first list is of three-letter words. Younger learners or those new to the English Language will find these words relatively easier to learn and remember. The next set of words are four letter words. It is important to know these words as they are often included in some entrance exams; especially the 11+ verbal reasoning tests. The third set of words have more letters and includes other useful words found in the Key Stage 1 to Key Stage 3 syllabi and beyond. Some words are more advanced and knowing them will increase your vocabulary and improve your communication skills. At the end of each list are some blank spaces for any notes you wish to make or other words you choose to add. If there is a word on the list that you don't know, use a good dictionary to find its meaning and start using it.

The lists of words include some that are more commonly used than others and some formal and informal words. Tick the words you know and learn those that are new to you. The use of all the practical resources provided at the back of the book will definitely help you to improve your word power. Follow these steps to improve your vocabulary and ability to remember the words you have learned.

- Read, Read, Read

The essential activities are reading, the use of a dictionary and recording the knowledge in a book like this one. In order to do this systematically, you will need a practical plan that works for you. Use the guide below to improve your vocabulary.

- Have A Plan

Choose a book to read periodically and decide on the number of pages you will read each day.

Reading will make you more familiar with words and increase the prospect of learning new words. Magazines, newspapers, novels, short stories are usually available in bookshops, libraries and online. Books are available in different genres and formats. They are now available as e-books, PDF's and can be downloaded to mobile devices. Books are either fiction or non-fiction and it is helpful to know the genre of the books you enjoy reading in order to develop and sustain the habit. Some common classification include: anthology, action and adventure, autobiographies, biographies, comedies, cookbooks, diaries, dictionaries, drama, encyclopaedias, fantasy, guides, health, history, horror, journals, mystery, poetry, prayer books, romance, satire, science fiction and trilogy.

- A Dictionary Is A Must Have And Must Use!

When you see a new word, make sure you understand the context of its use. Your knowledge of root words, parts of speech, prefixes, suffixes, spelling rules, synonyms and antonyms should prove helpful in understanding its meaning. Look up the word in a good dictionary.

A good dictionary is essential so buy or download a dictionary app to a mobile device or borrow one from a library. Make sure that the type of dictionary is right for your purposes. A teacher or librarian will be able to give some advice on a suitable dictionary to buy. A dictionary provides examples of how to use a word and a guide to its pronunciation, origin and any associated synonym or antonym are often stated.

- Use the dictionary to search for, or confirm the correct spelling of a word and its various forms. The adjective, adverb, verb, and noun forms of a word are given. Abbreviations are stated beside each word to denote its part of speech. For example: adjective *(adj.)*; adverb *(adv.)*; conjunction *(conj.)*; interjection *(interj.)*; noun*(n)*; preposition *(prep.)*; pronoun *(pron.)* and verb *(vb.)*.

- Use the dictionary to clarify the meaning of each new word you come across. After you have checked the dictionary and learnt the word, add the word to the relevant list in this book so that you can quickly refer to it when required. After you have recorded it, follow the practical steps below so that you will always remember it:
  - learn the spelling, meaning, parts of speech of the new word. Appendix 5 is a template of a form you can use.

  - note down the sentence in which the word was used and write your own sentence, using that word. Appendix 7 is an example of a template that is useful for this purpose.
  - include the word in your conversations.
  - Keeping a journal is a good habit to have.
  - seize every opportunity to practice using the word as often as possible.

You will notice an improvement in your vocabulary and ability to communicate more effectively.

i.   Alphabetical Lists of Useful Words

Learn and use the words listed below. When you have learnt all the words of each alphabet, tick the summary sheet in Appendix 1 to record your progress.

A a is For Alpha *(Phonetic Alphabet)*

Words Beginning With The Letter **A**

Three Letter Words

ace act add ado age ago aid ail aim air ale all amp
and ant any ape apt arc are ark arm art ash ask ass
auk awe awl axe

Four Letter Words

able ache acid acne acre ages aide aims airy ajar
ally aloe alps also amps anew anon arch area arid
arms army arts atom aunt aura avid avow away

Words With More Letters

aardvark	affirmation	ancestry	approximate	asylum
abandon	afford	anchor	aquarium	asymmetric
abbreviation	afforestation	ancient	arbitrary	atheism
aberrant	afraid	anemone	archaeology	athlete
abhorrent	aggravate	anguish	archaic	athletics
abracadabra	aggression	annihilate	archangel	atmosphere
abrogate	aghast	annihilation	archbishop	atrocious
abrupt	agnosticism	anniversary	archetype	atrocity
abscess	agoraphobia	announce	architect	attached
abscond	agreeable	announcement	arduous	attendant
absence	aisle	annoyance	argument	attention
absorb	alfresco	annulment	aristocracy	attenuate
absurd	algae	anonymous	aristocratic	attic
accelerate	alibis	antagonist	arithmetic	attitude
accent	alignment	antelope	aromatic	attribute
acceptance	allege	antennae	arrange	attrition
accident	allergic	anthropologist	arrive	aubergine

Vocabulary: The personal Dictionary

acclamation	alligator	antibiotic	artichoke	auburn
accompany	allotment	antithesis	articulate	auctioneer
accomplish	allowance	antonym	artist	audacious
accountant	alphabet	anxiety	ascend	audible
achieve	alteration	apartheid	ascension	audience
acknowledge	although	apathetic	asparagus	audition
acquaintance	aluminium	apologise	asphalt	augment
acquiescence	always	apostle	asphyxiate	augur
acquire	amalgam	apostrophe	asphyxiation	aural
acquit	amateur	appalled	aspiration	auspicious
acrimonious	amaze	apparatus	assailant	austere
adequate	ambidextrous	apparel	assassin	authentic
adieu	ambiguous	apparent	assault	author
adjacent	ambivalent	appeal	assembly	automatic
admissible	amethyst	appearance	assertion	automation
admittance	ammunition	appease	assessment	autopilot
admonition	among	appellant	assignment	autumn
adolescence	amorous	appendage	assistance	auxiliary
advantage	amphibious	appetite	assorted	available
advantageous	anaesthetic	applause	assumption	avarice
adversary	analogy	appraisal	asteroid	avaricious
aerate	analyse	appreciate	asthma	aversion
aerial	analysis	apprehend	asthmatic	avocado
aesthetic	anarchist	apprentice	astringent	awful
affection	anarchy	appropriate	astronaut	awkward
affiliation	ancestor	approval	astute	azure

B b is For Bravo *(Phonetic Alphabet)*

Words Beginning With The Letter **B**

Three Letter Words

baa bad bag bah bam ban bar bat bay bed bee beg bet bey bib bid
big bin bio bit boa bob boo bop bow box boy bra bub bud bug bum
bun bus but buy bye

Four Letter Words

bail	bait	bake	bald	bale	balk	balm	band	bang	bank
bare	bark	barn	base	bash	bask	bass	bate	bawl	bead
beak	beam	bean	beef	beep	belt	bend	bent	berg	bike
blot	blow	blue	blur	boar	boat	body	boil	bold	bolt
bomb	bond	bone	boom	bore	born	boss	both	bowl	bran
bulb	bulk	bull	bump	bunk	buoy	burg	burn	bury	bush
bust	busy	butt	buzz	byte					

Words With More Letters

babble	baste	bilingual	bounce	bronchitis
baboon	battalion	binary	boundary	bronze
bachelor	bazaar	binge	bountiful	broom
bacteria	beach	binoculars	bounty	brought
badger	beatitude	biography	bourgeois	bruised
baggage	beautiful	biotic	boutique	brunch
bailiff	because	birthday	boycott	brusque
balance	become	biscuit	bracket	brutal
balance	bedraggled	blackboard	braille	buccaneer
balderdash	before	blanched	brassiere	bucket
ballast	begin	blancmange	brawl	buckle
ballerina	beginning	blasphemy	brazen	budgerigar
ballet	begrudge	bleary	bread	budget
balloon	beguile	blemish	breadth	budgie

Vocabulary: The personal Dictionary

bamboozle	behaviour	blitz	breakfast	buffalo
banal	being	bloated	breakfast	buffeted
bandage	beleaguer	blossom	breathalyser	bulge
banishment	believe	blouse	breed	bulldozer
bankrupt	belligerent	bludgeon	brick	bulletin
bankruptcy	benefit	blunder	bridal	bumptious
banquet	benefitted	board	bride	bungalow
barbarian	benevolent	bodily	bridge	buoyancy
barbecue	benign	bombardment	bridle	buoyant
bargain	bequeath	bondage	brief	bureau
barometer	beret	bonfire	brief	bureaucracy
barren	berserk	bongo	briers	business
barricade	besiege	bonkers	brilliant	butterfly
barrister	betrayal	boredom	broach	
basically	better	borough	broadcast	
basil	between	bottle	broccoli	
bastard	biceps	bough	brochure	

C c is For Charlie *(Phonetic Alphabet)*

Words Beginning With The Letter **C**

Three Letter Words

cab cad can cap car cat cob cod cog con coo cop cot
cow cox coy cry cub cud cue cup cur cut

Four Letter Words

cafe cage cake calf call calm camp cane cape card
care carp cart case cash cast cave cell cent chap
chat chef chic chin chip chop city clad clam clan
clap claw clay clef clip clop clot club clue coal
coat coca cock coil coin coke cola cold colt coma
comb come cone cook cool coop cope copy cord core
cork corn cost coup cove crab cram crew crib crop
crow cube cuff cult curd cure curl cute cyan

Words With More Letters

cackle	celery	clench	concurrent	convulsion
cacophony	celestial	clientele	concussion	cooperate
cadaver	celibacy	climb	condemnation	cooperative
cafeteria	cellophane	clinched	condiment	coordination
caffeine	Celsius	clique	condone	coquette
cajole	cemetery	clothes	conduit	corduroy
calamity	centenary	clothing	confectionary	coriander
calculation	centennial	cloves	confederate	Corinthians
calendar	centilitre	coagulate	conference	corkscrew
calligraphy	century	coalesce	confetti	cornerstone
callous	cereal	cocoa	confidential	corporation
cameraman	cerebral	coconut	confiscate	corpse
camouflage	ceremony	coerce	confiscation	correction
campaign	certain	coffee	confluence	correlate
cancellation	cessation	cognizant	confound	correspond
cancerous	challenge	collaborate	congeal	correspondence
candidate	chamomile	collar	conglomerate	corrosive

Vocabulary: The personal Dictionary

candour	champagne	collateral	congratulation	corruption
cannabis	champion	colleague	congregation	cosmos
cannibal	chancellor	collect	congruent	costume
canonical	changeable	collegiate	conjecture	countenance
cantankerous	channel	collide	conjoint	counterfeit
canvas	chaotic	colloquial	conjunctivitis	country
canvassing	character	colloquy	conned	courageous
capable	charitable	colonel	connoisseur	courteous
capacious	charlatan	colonialism	conquer	courtesy
capillary	chasm	colony	conquest	covenant
capitalist	chauffeur	colossal	conscience	coward
capitulate	chauvinist	combatant	conscientious	coyote
cappuccino	chemist	combination	conscious	crave
capricious	cherish	commandeer	consecrate	crawl
captain	chieftain	commander	conservative	create
capture	chilblain	commemorate	consideration	creation
caravan	chimpanzee	commence	consign	creek
carbohydrate	chintz	commendable	consignment	creep
carburettor	chiropody	comment	consistency	crescent
cardigan	chiropractor	commentator	consistent	criminal
career	chisel	commercial	consolation	crimson
caress	chivalry	commiserate	conspicuous	cringe
cargo	choir	commission	conspiracy	crinkle
caricature	choreographer	commissionaire	constellation	criticism
carnage	choreography	committee	constituent	crucible
carnivore	Christmas	communion	constitution	crucify
carriage	chronic	communism	construe	crumbs
carriage	chronicle	companion	consultant	crusade
carry	chrysanthemum	comparative	consummate	crustacean
cartoonist	church	comparison	contagious	crypt
cashew	churn	compartment	contaminate	crystal
cashier	chutney	compassion	contamination	crystalline
cassette	cigarette	compatibility	contemplate	cucumber
castanets	cinch	compelled	contemporary	culpable
castigate	cinema	competent	contention	culprit
casualty	cinnamon	competitive	continent	cumin
cataclysmic	circuit	complaisant	contingency	curfew
catalogue	circuitous	completely	contract	curious
catarrh	circumference	component	contradict	currency
catastrophe	circumspect	composure	contradictory	cursory
catch	circumstance	compound	contrite	custom
catechism	circumvent	compromise	controversial	customary

category	cistern	computer	conundrum	customer
catholic	citizen	conceal	convalesce	cyanide
catnap	civilian	conceit	convenience	cyclone
cauliflower	civilization	conceive	converge	cylinder
caustic	claim	concentration	convert	cynic
cautionary	clandestine	concession	convey	cynicism
ceiling	claustrophobia	conciliation	convince	cynosure
celebrate	clean	conclave	convocation	cypress
celebrity	clear	concoct	convoy	

Vocabulary: The personal Dictionary

D d is For Delta *(Phonetic Alphabet)*

Words Beginning With The Letter **D**

Three Letter Words

dab	dad	dam	day	den	dew	dib	did	die	dig	dim	din	dip
doe	dog	don	doo	dot	dry	dub	dud	due	dug	dun	duo	dux
dye										

Four Letter Words

daft	dame	damn	damp	dare	dark	darn	dart	dash	data
date	daub	dawn	daze	dead	deaf	deal	dear	debt	deck
deed	deem	deep	deer	dell	dent	deny	desk	dial	dice
diet	dime	dine	dire	dirt	disc	dish	dive	dock	dodo
dome	doom	door	dope	dorm	dose	dote	dove	down	doze
drab	drag	draw	dray	drip	drop	drug	drum	dual	duck
duel	duet	duke	dull	dumb	dump	dune	dupe	dunk	dusk
dust	duty	dyed							

Words With More Letters

dachshund	deliberate	detriment	disbelief	divulge
daffodil	delicacy	deuce	disburse	docile
dahlia	delicatessen	Deuteronomy	discard	doctor
damage	delicious	devastation	discern	doctrine
damnation	delight	develop	discharge	documentary
dandruff	delinquent	development	discipline	dodge
dangerous	delirious	deviation	discontent	doggerel
dangle	deluge	devious	discourse	dollar
daredevil	delusion	devote	discover	dolphin
daughter	demagogue	devotion	discreet	domicile
deadlock	demarcate	devour	discrete	domination
debate	demeanour	dexterous	discriminate	domineering
debauch	dementia	diagnosis	discursive	dominoes
debauched	democracy	diagonal	discus	donate
debilitate	demography	dialogue	discuss	donor
debility	demon	dialogue	discussion	doomed

debonair	demonstration	diameter	disease	dormant
debris	denigrate	diamond	disgruntled	double
debtor	denounce	diary	disguise	doubt
decadence	denouncement	diatribe	disgust	doubtful
deceit	denunciation	dictation	dishwasher	dough
deceive	dependence	dictator	disingenuous	dowdy
decency	deplorable	diction	disintegrate	downcast
decide	deport	different	dismantle	dozen
deciduous	depository	differentiate	dismissal	draft
decimal	deprave	difficult	disobedient	dragooned
decimate	depreciate	digger	disorganise	drain
decipher	deprive	digitisation	disparaging	drastically
decisive	depth	dignify	disparity	draughts
declaration	depth	dignitary	disperse	draughty
decline	derailment	dignity	dispose	dream
decomposes	derelict	digress	disputable	drenched
decorate	dermatitis	dilapidate	disrupt	dresses
decorum	derogatory	dilate	dissatisfied	dribble
decoy	descend	dilemma	disseminate	drooled
dedicate	description	diligent	dissent	drudgery
defamatory	desert	dilute	dissimilar	drunkard
default	desiccate	diminished	dissipated	drunkenness
defer	desirable	diminutive	dissipation	dubious
defiant	desire	dimwit	dissociate	dugong
definite	desirous	dinosaur	dissolute	dumbfounded
deflate	desperate	diplomacy	dissuade	dunce
deflect	destination	diplomat	dissuade	dungarees
deform	destiny	direction	distilled	dungeon
defraud	destroy	director	distillery	duplex
defunct	detach	dirtiness	distinguish	duress
degenerate	detachable	disagreeable	distraught	dutiful
degradable	detergent	disappear	disuse	dwarf
dehydrate	determination	disappoint	diverge	dynamite
deign	deterred	disapprove	diversity	dysentery
deity	deterrence	disarray	divine	dyspepsia

Vocabulary: The personal Dictionary

delectable	deterrent	disaster	divisible
delete	detour	disastrous	divorce

E e is For Echo *(Phonetic Alphabet)*

Words Beginning With The Letter **E**

Three Letter Words

ear   eat   ebb   eel   egg   ego   eke   elf   elk   elm   emu   end   era
err   eve   ewe   eye

Four Letter Words

each   earl   earn   ease   east   echo   edge   edit   else   emir
emit   envy   epic   euro   even   ever   exam   exit

Words With More Letters

eager	elixir	enormous	escalate	executive
eardrum	elocution	enough	escape	exemplify
early	eloquence	enquiry	escarpment	exhale
earmark	elucidate	enrich	especially	exhaust
earnest	emancipate	enrol	espionage	exhausted
earthquake	embarrass	enslave	essay	exhibit
Easter	embarrassment	ensuing	essential	exhilarated
eaves	embellish	ensure	establish	exigent
eavesdrop	embezzled	entailed	esteem	exile
ebbing	emblem	entertainer	estimate	existence
ebullient	embrace	enthusiasm	estrange	Exodus
eccentric	embryo	enthusiastic	eternity	exonerate
ecclesiastic	emerald	entice	ethereal	exorbitant
echidna	emerge	entire	ethical	expand
eclipse	emergence	entity	ethics	expanse
economical	eminence	entourage	etiquette	expatriate
economist	eminent	entrenched	eucalyptus	expect
economy	emolument	entrepreneur	eulogise	expedient
ecstasy	emphatic	enumerate	euphoria	expend
ecstatic	employ	enunciate	European	expenses

Vocabulary: The personal Dictionary

eczema	employer	envelope	euthanasia	experience
edge	emporium	envious	evacuate	experiment
edify	empty	ephemeral	evade	explain
education	emulate	epicurean	evaluate	explanation
effect	enable	epidemic	evangelical	explicit
effective	enact	epidermis	evaporate	explode
effervescent	enchanting	epilepsy	evasion	exploit
efficacious	enclose	epileptic	evening	explore
efficient	encounter	episode	eventual	expose
effloresce	encourage	epistle	eviction	expressive
effortless	encyclopaedia	epitome	evidence	exquisite
effrontery	endeavour	epoch	evolution	extension
effuse	endorse	eponymous	exaggerate	extinction
egoist	endurance	equality	exalt	extinguish
either	endure	equanimity	examination	extra
eject	enemy	equate	example	extract
ejection	energetic	equation	excavate	extracurricular
elaborate	energy	equator	excellent	extraneous
elation	enervate	equatorial	except	extraordinary
elder	engineer	equip	excessive	extravagant
electrician	engineer	equipment	exchange	extremely
elegance	engorge	equivalent	excitement	extremist
elementary	engrave	equivocate	exciting	extricate
elephant	enhance	eradicate	exclaim	extrinsic
elevation	enigma	erase	exclude	extrovert
elicit	enjoyable	errand	exclusive	exuberant
eligible	enlighten	erratic	excrete	exude
eliminate	enlist	erroneous	excruciating	
eliminated	enmity	erudite	excursion	
elitist	ennui	erupt	excuse	

F f is For Foxtrot *(Phonetic Alphabet)*

Words Beginning With The Letter **F**

Three Letter Words

fab	fad	fan	far	fat	fax	fay	fed	fee	fen	few	fey	fez
fib	fig	fin	fir	fit	fix	fly	fob	foe	fog	fop	for	fox
fry	fun	fur								

Four Letter Words

face	fact	fade	fail	fair	fake	fall	fame	fang	fare
farm	fast	fate	fawn	fear	feat	feed	feel	feet	fell
felt	fend	file	fill	film	find	fine	fire	firm	firs
fish	fist	five	flag	flap	flat	flaw	flay	flea	flee
flip	flog	flop	flow	foal	foam	foil	fold	folk	fond
font	food	fool	foot	ford	fork	form	fort	foul	four
fowl	fray	fret	frog	from	fuel	full	fume	fund	fury
fuse	fuss								

Words With More Letters

fable	feasible	finance	foggy	frailty
fabric	feature	finesse	foible	frame
fabricate	federation	fisticuffs	folklore	frank
fabulous	feeble	fixation	follow	frantic
facet	feeler	fizzle	foolish	fraternity
facetious	feeling	fjord	forbearance	fraud
facilitate	feign	flabbergast	forbid	fraudulent
facsimile	feint	flaccid	force	freak
factitious	feline	flagrance	forearm	freeze
factor	fellowship	flamboyant	forecast	freight
factory	felony	flame	forehead	friend
factual	female	flammable	foreign	frightened
faculty	femininity	flannelette	forensic	frigid
Fahrenheit	ferment	flare	forest	frill

Vocabulary: The personal Dictionary

failed	ferocious	flash	foretell	fringe
failure	fertile	flatten	forfeit	frivolous
faint	fervour	flattery	forgery	frock
faithful	festive	flatulent	forgetful	front
fallacious	fetish	flaunted	forgotten	froth
fallacy	feverish	fledgling	format	frown
fallible	fiasco	fleet	formidable	frugal
falter	fibre	flexible	formulaic	fruit
family	fiction	flimsy	forsaken	fugitive
famous	fictitious	flinch	fortitude	fulfilled
fanatic	fiddle	flirt	fortuitous	fumble
fancy	fidelity	float	fortuity	function
fantastic	fidgety	flock	fortunate	fungi
farce	field	flood	forty	funny
farcical	fielder	floor	fossil	furbish
fascinate	fiend	flounder	foundation	furious
fascism	fierce	flour	foundry	further
fastidious	fiery	flourish	fount	fuselage
fatal	fifteen	fluent	fountain	fusion
fatality	fight	fluid	fourteen	fussy
father	figment	flummox	fracas	futile
fathom	figure	fluorescence	fraction	future
fatigue	filament	fluoridate	fracture	fuzzy
faulty	filial	flush	fragile	
favourite	filthy	fluster	fragment	
fearful	final	flutter	fragrance	

G g is For Golf *(Phonetic Alphabet)*

Words Beginning With The Letter <u>G</u>

Three Letter Words

gab gag gal gap gas gay gee gel gem get gig gin god
got gum gun gut guy gym

Four Letter Words

gain gala gale game gang gape garb gash gasp gate
gaze gear geek gems gene germ gift girl give glad
glee glop glow glue glug glum glut gnat gnaw goal
goat gods gold golf gong good goof goon gore gosh
gown grab gram grey grid grim grin grip grit grow
grub gulf gulp gung gush gust

Words With More Letters

gabble	geography	gloomy	grant	group
gadget	geology	glorify	grasp	grovelled
gaiety	gerbil	gluttonous	grassland	grudge
galaxy	germinate	glycerine	grate	gruel
gallant	gesticulate	glycogen	gratification	gruesome
gallivant	gesture	gnarled	gratitude	grumpy
galvanise	ghastly	gnash	gratuitous	grunge
gamble	ghetto	goalkeeper	gratuity	grunt
garage	ghoulish	goggle	gravel	guarantee
gargantuan	giant	goitre	gravity	guarantor
garlic	gibberish	goodness	graze	guard
garment	giddy	goose	great	guardian
garnish	gigantic	gorgeous	greengrocer	guess
garrison	gimmick	gorilla	greet	guest
garrotted	ginger	gossip	gregarious	guide
gateau	giraffe	gouge	grief	guild
gauche	girdle	govern	grievance	guillotine
gaudy	glacier	government	grieve	guilty
gauge	gladioli	grace	grievous	guinea

Vocabulary: The personal Dictionary

gaunt	glamorous	gradation	grimace	guise
gazetteer	glamour	gradient	grind	guitar
gecko	glance	gradual	gripe	gullible
geisha	glare	graffiti	grisly	gumption
generate	glasshouse	graft	gritty	gutsy
generic	glaze	grain	groceries	guzzle
generosity	gleam	grammar	groom	gymkhana
Genesis	glide	grammatical	groove	gymnasium
genius	glimpse	grand	gross	gymnast
genteel	glisten	grandeur	grotesque	gyrate
gentle	glitter	grandiose	grouch	
genuine	global	granite	ground	

H h is For Hotel *(Phonetic Alphabet)*

Words Beginning With The Letter <u>H</u>

Three Letter Words

had hag ham has hat hay hem hen her hew hex hey hid him
hip hit hoe hog hop hot how hoy hub hue hug huh hum hut

Four Letter Words

hack	haft	hail	hair	half	hall	halo	halt	hand	hang
hard	hare	harm	harp	hash	hate	have	hawk	haze	head
heal	heap	hear	heat	heel	heir	help	herb	herd	here
hero	hide	high	hike	hill	hilt	hind	hint	hire	hiss
hive	hoax	hold	hole	holy	home	hood	hoof	hook	hoot
hope	horn	hose	host	hour	howl	huff	huge	hula	hulk
hull	hump	hung	hunt	hurl	hurt	hush	hymn		

Words With More Letters

habit	harmony	heinous	hoard	hullabaloo
habitation	harpoon	helicopter	hoarse	humanitarian
haemoglobin	harrowing	helter-skelter	hocus-pocus	humdrum
haemorrhage	harsh	hemisphere	hodgepodge	humiliate
Haggai	harvest	herbaceous	hoist	humility
haggard	hassle	herculean	hoity-toity	humour
haggle	haste	hereditary	holiday	humorous
halcyon	hatred	heritage	holocaust	hungry
hallow	haughty	hermetic	homage	hurricane
hallucination	haunt	heroism	homicide	hurry
hammer	havoc	hesitate	homonym	hurtful
hammered	hazard	heterogeneous	honcho	hurtle
hammock	headquarter	hiatus	honest	hush-hush
hamstring	headstrong	hiccough	honky-tonk	hustler
handcuff	health	hideous	honorarium	hydrogen
handful	heard	hierarchy	honorary	hypochondriac
handicap	hearsay	hieroglyphics	honour	hypocrisy
handicraft	hearse	higgledy-piggledy	hooligan	hypocrite

Vocabulary: The personal Dictionary

handkerchief	heart	highbrow	hopeful	hypothesis
handsome	heave	highly	horizon	hysterical
happened	heaven	highway	horrendous	
harangue	heavy	hijack	horrible	
harass	Hebrew	hilarious	horrify	
harassment	heckle	hinder	hospice	
hardly	hectic	hindrance	hospital	
harlequin	height	hippopotamus	hotel	
harlot	heighten	history	house	

I i is For India *(Phonetic Alphabet)*

Words Beginning With The Letter **I**

Three Letter Words

ice ick icy ilk ill imp ink inn ion ire irk its

Four Letter Words

icon idea idle idol iffy inch into iris iron isle itch item

Words With More Letters

icicle	impart	incision	inexhaustible	insipid
ideal	impartial	incisive	inexorable	insolvent
idealistic	impatient	inclination	inexpensive	inspection
ideally	impeccable	include	inextricable	inspire
identical	impede	inclusion	infallible	instant
identify	impediment	incognito	infamous	instantaneous
identity	impenitent	incomparable	infant	instead
ideological	imperative	incompetent	infatuate	instinct
idiosyncrasy	imperfect	incomprehensible	inferior	instruction
ignite	impersonal	inconceivable	infertile	instrument
ignition	impertinence	incongruous	infidelity	insubordinate
ignoble	impetuous	inconspicuous	infiltrate	insufficient
ignominious	impetus	incontinence	infinite	insulate
ignorance	impinge	incredible	infirmity	insult
ignorant	implicate	incriminate	inflammable	insurgence
ignore	implicit	inculcate	inflate	insurrection
illegal	imply	indefatigable	inflationary	intangible
illegible	impolite	indefinite	inflict	integrate
illegitimacy	important	indelible	influence	integrity

Vocabulary: The personal Dictionary

illegitimate	impose	indemnify	influential	intellect
illiberal	impossible	indent	informal	intellectual
illicit	impotence	independent	information	intelligence
illiterate	impoverish	index	infrequent	intense
illogical	impractical	indicate	infringement	interdict
illuminate	impregnable	indication	infuriate	interest
illusion	impress	indices	ingenious	interfere
illustrate	impression	indict	ingratiate	interlope
illustration	imprison	indifference	ingredient	intermediate
illustrious	improbable	indigenous	inhabit	intermission
image	impromptu	indigent	inhabitant	intermittent
imagination	impropriety	indigestible	inhalation	internal
imaginative	improvement	indignant	inhale	international
imagine	impulse	indignity	inherent	interpretation
imbecile	impurity	indirect	inheritance	interrogate
imbibe	impute	indispensable	inhibit	interrupt
imitation	inability	individual	inhibition	interval
immaculate	inaccurate	indoctrinate	inimitable	interview
immature	inadequacy	indomitable	iniquitous	intestine
immeasurable	inadvertent	induce	initiate	intimacy
immediate	inapt	induction	injection	introduce
immemorial	inattentive	indulge	injunction	irascible
immense	inaugural	industrious	innate	irrelevant
immerse	inauspicious	indwelling	innings	irreparable
immersion	incalculable	inebriate	innocent	irreplaceable
immigrant	incandescent	ineffable	innocuous	irresistible
immigrate	incapable	ineffective	innovation	irresponsible
immigration	incarcerate	inefficient	innuendo	irrevocable
imminence	incarnation	ineligible	inoculate	italicize
immortal	incense	inept	inordinate	itinerant
immune	inception	inert	inquisition	itinerary
impact	inchoate	inescapable	insalubrious	
impairment	incident	inevitable	insincere	
impalpable	incidentally	inexcusable	insinuate	

J j is For Juliet *(Phonetic Alphabet)*

Words Beginning With The Letter **J**

Three Letter Words

jab   jag   jam   jap   jar   jaw   jay   jet   Jew   jib   jig   job   joe
jog   jot   joy   jug   jut

Four Letter Words

jade   jail   java   jazz   jean   jeep   jeer   jerk   jest   jibe
jinx   jive   join   joke   jolt   judo   jump   junk   jury   just

Words With More Letters

jackal	jeopardy	jockey	joyful	juncture
jackass	jester	jodhpurs	jubilant	jungle
jacket	Jesus	joggle	judge	junior
jaguar	jettison	joined	judicious	jurisdiction
jam-pack	jewel	joint	juggernaut	justice
January	jeweller	jollity	juggle	justification
jargon	jewellery	journal	jugular	juvenile
jaundice	jigsaw	journalist	juice	
jealous	jittery	journey	jumble	
jeopardize	jobless	jovial	junction	

K k is For Kilo *(Phonetic Alphabet)*

Words Beginning With The Letter **K**

Three Letter Words

keg	key	kid	kin	kit

Four Letter Words

keel	keen	keep	kelp	kept	kerb	kick	kill	kiln	kilo kilt
kind	king	kiss	kite	kiwi	knee	knit	knob	knot	know

Words With More Letters

kaleidoscopic	kidnapped	kindred	knack	knock
kangaroo	kidney	kiosk	knead	knowledge
karate	killed	kitchen	kneel	knowledgeable
keenness	kilometre	kitchenette	knick-knack	knuckle
kettle	kindergarten	kitten	knife	kudos
khaki	kindness	kleptomania	knight	

L l is For Lima *(Phonetic Alphabet)*

Words Beginning With The Letter **L**

Three Letter Words

lab	lad	lag	lap	law	lax	lay	lea	led	leg	let	lid	lie
lip	lit	lob	log	loo	lot	low	lug	lux	lye			

Four Letter Words

lace	lack	lady	lair	lake	lamb	lame	lamp	land	lane
lard	lark	lash	last	late	laud	lava	lawn	lazy	lead
leaf	leak	lean	leap	leek	left	lend	lens	less	lice
lick	lido	life	lift	like	lily	limb	lime	line	link
lint	lion	lira	lisp	list	live	load	loaf	loan	lock
loft	logo	loin	long	look	loom	loop	loot	lord	lost
loud	love	luck	lull	lump	lung	lure	lurk	lush	lynx

Words With More Letters

label	laundered	length	limitation	lonely
laboratory	launderette	lenient	limousine	longitude
laborious	laundry	leopard	lineage	lorgnette
labour	lavender	lesson	linen	lottery
labourer	lavish	lethargy	lingerie	lounge
labyrinth	lawbreaker	lettuce	linguist	lousy
lackadaisical	lawful	leukaemia	lioness	loyal
lacklustre	lawlessness	levelled	liqueur	lozenge
ladies	lawsuit	leverage	liquid	lucidity
ladle	lawyer	lewdness	liquidate	lucrative
laggard	layette	lexicon	liquor	lucre
lamentable	leader	liability	literal	luggage
lamingtons	league	liaise	literate	lugubrious
landscape	leanness	liaison	literature	lukewarm
language	learn	libellous	litre	lumber

Vocabulary: The personal Dictionary

languish	learn	liberal	little	luminous
languor	leather	liberty	liturgical	luminous
languorous	leaven	library	liturgy	lunacy
lapse	lecturer	license	livelihood	lunch
laryngitis	ledger	licentious	lizard	lupus
larynx	leech	lieutenant	loaded	lurid
lassitude	legal	lifeless	loathe	luscious
later	legend	lifetime	local	lustre
lather	legend	ligament	locality	luxurious
latitude	legend	light	location	luxury
lattice	legendary	lightheaded	lodgings	lymphatic
laudation	legion	lightning	loftiest	lyric
laugh	legislation	lightweight	logical	
laughter	legitimacy	lilac	loiter	
launch	leisure	Lilliputian	loneliness	

M m is For Mother *(Phonetic Alphabet)*

Words Beginning With The Letter <u>M</u>

Three Letter Words

mac mad mag man map mar mat maw max may men met mic
mid mix mob mod mom moo mop mow mud mug mum

Four Letter Words

mace maid mail main make male mall malt mane many
mare mark mash mast mate maze mead meal mean meat
meet melt mend menu meow mesh mess mice mild mile
milk mill mime mind mine mint miss mist moan moat
mock mode mole monk mono mood moon moor mope more
morn moss most moth move mown mows much mule mull
muse mush muss musk must mute myth

Words With More Letters

macabre	manipulate	medicine	metropolis	moderate
macadamia	manmade	mediocre	metropolitan	modern
Machiavellian	mannerism	meditate	midday	modest
machination	manoeuvre	Mediterranean	midnight	modesty
machine	mantle	medium	migration	moisture
machinery	manufacture	melancholic	milieu	molecule
machinist	manumit	melancholy	militant	molecule
maelstrom	manure	mellow	military	mollycoddle
maestro	maraud	melodic	milkshake	momentary
magazine	margin	melodious	millennium	momentum
maggot	marginal	melodramatic	million	monastery
magic	marijuana	member	millionaire	money
magical	marina	membership	mimicry	monkey
magician	marinate	memoir	minced	monopoly
magnanimous	mariner	memorandum	mineral	monotone

Vocabulary: The personal Dictionary

magnate	maritime	memorial	miniature	monstrosity
magnetic	maroon	memorise	minimal	month
magnetism	marriage	memory	minimum	monument
magnificent	marshal	memory	minister	moonstruck
magnify	marvellous	menace	ministerial	morale
magnitude	masculine	menial	minor	mortgaged
mainframe	masquerade	mental	minority	mortality
mainstream	massacre	mentality	minute	mortgage
maintain	massive	mention	minutiae	mortuary
maintenance	master	mentor	miraculous	mosquito
majesty	masterpiece	mercantile	misanthrope	motivation
majority	masticate	mercenary	misappropriation	mountain
makeshift	match	merchandise	misbehave	mouthpiece
maladjusted	material	merchant	miscellaneous	movement
malady	materialistic	mercurial	mischief	mudslinging
malaise	matrimony	mercy	mischievous	mulish
malapert	matter	merge	misconstrue	multifaceted
malefactor	mature	merger	misdemeanour	multiplicity
malevolent	mausoleum	meridian	miserable	mundane
malice	mauve	merit	mishmash	murky
malign	maximum	meritorious	misogynous	murmur
malignant	meagre	merriment	mission	muscle
malleable	meagrely	mesmerises	missionary	muscular
mammal	meander	message	mistake	mushroom
mammoth	meaningful	metallic	misunderstand	mustard
mandate	measure	metamorphic	misuse	mutilate
mandatory	measurement	metamorphosis	mitigate	mutiny
manhandle	mechanical	metanoia	mitten	myriad
maniac	medal	meteor	mnemonic	mysterious
manifestation	meddle	meteoric	moccasin	
manifesto	median	methodological	mockery	
manifold	mediator	meticulous	model	

N n is For **November** *(Phonetic Alphabet)*

Words Beginning With The Letter <u>N</u>

Three Letter Words

nab	nag	nap	nay	nee	neo	net	new	nib	nil	nip	nit	nix
nob	nod	nog	nor	not	now	nub	nun	nut				

Four Letter Words

nail	name	naps	navy	near	neat	neck	need	neon	nest
newt	next	nice	nine	none	noon	nose	nude	numb	

Words With More Letters

naïve	necklace	niche	noodle	nugget
naked	needle	niece	north	nuisance
narcissism	negative	nifty	nostril	number
narrate	neglect	niggle	notable	numerate
narrative	negligence	night	noticeable	numerous
narrow	negotiate	nightmare	notify	nuptial
nasty	neighbour	nimble	notion	nurse
nation	neither	ninth	notorious	nursery
native	nephew	nippy	nourish	nurture
natural	Neptune	nitwit	novel	nutriment
naughty	netball	nocturnal	novelty	nutritious
nauseate	nettle	noise	novice	
nautical	network	nomadic	noxious	
navigate	neurotic	nominee	nozzle	
nearly	neutral	nonpartisan	nuance	
nebulous	neutralise	nonplus	nucleus	
necessary	newcomer	nonsense	nudge	
necessity	nexus	nonsensical	nudity	

O o is For Oscar *(Phonetic Alphabet)*

Words Beginning With The Letter <u>O</u>

Three Letter Words

oaf   oak   oar   oat   odd   ode   off   oft   oil   old   ole   one   opt
ore   our   out   ova   owe   owl   own

Four Letter Words

obey   oboe   ogle   ogre   omit   once   only   onus   onyx   open
oral   orca   ouch   ours   oval   oven   oxen

Words With More Letters

obedience	occasion	ominous	oracle	outfit
obeisance	occasionally	omission	orator	outlandish
obese	occult	omnipresent	orbit	outlaw
obituary	occupancy	omniscient	orchard	outlook
object	occupation	omnivorous	orchestra	outmanoeuvre
objective	occupier	onerous	orchid	outrage
obligate	occupy	onomatopoeia	ordeal	outrageous
obligation	occur	opaque	order	outside
oblique	occurrence	opened	ordinance	outspoken
obliterate	ocean	openness	oregano	outweigh
oblivion	octogenarian	operate	organ	overall
obloquy	odious	operator	organise	overdraft
obnoxious	odorous	ophthalmic	orienteering	overlook
obscene	odour	opinion	orifice	overpower
obscenity	offence	opinionated	origin	overrate
obscure	offend	opium	original	oversee
observance	offender	opponent	originate	overtake
observatory	offer	opportunity	ornament	overthrow
observe	offering	oppose	ornate	overturn
obsessive	office	opposite	orthodox	overview
obsolescence	officer	opposition	orthopaedic	ownership
obsolete	official	oppress	oscillate	oxidise
obstacle	officious	oppression	ostentatious	oxygen

obstetrician	offset	optic	ostracise	oyster
obstinate	offside	optical	ostracism	
obstruct	offspring	optician	ostrich	
obstruction	often	optimistic	other	
obtuse	olfaction	optometrist	ounce	
obvious	olfactory	opulent	outburst	

Vocabulary: The personal Dictionary

P p is For Peter *(Phonetic Alphabet)*

Words Beginning With The Letter **P**

Three Letter Words

pad	pal	pan	pap	par	pat	paw	pay	pea	pee	peg	pen	pep
per	pet	pew	pic	pie	pig	pin	pip	pit	ply	Pod	poo	pop
pot	pow	pox	pro	pry	pub	pug	pun	pup	put			

Four Letter Words

pace	pack	page	pail	pain	pair	pale	palm	pane	pant
park	part	pass	past	path	pave	peak	pear	peat	peck
peel	peen	peep	peer	pelt	perk	perm	pest	phew	pick
pier	pile	pill	pine	pink	pipe	pity	plan	play	plea
plot	plug	plum	plus	poem	poet	poke	pole	polo	pond
pony	pool	poor	pope	pore	pork	port	pose	posh	pour
pram	pray	prep	prey	prop	pull	pump	puny	pure	push
puss									

Words With More Letters

pacific	paternal	phial	portrait	profit
pacifist	pathetic	philanthropic	portray	profiteering
pacify	pathology	Philippians	positive	profound
package	patience	philistine	possess	prognosis
pagan	patient	phlegm	possession	prohibit
pageant	patriarch	phlegmatic	possibility	projection
painkiller	patron	phoenix	posterior	proliferate
painstaking	patronize	photographic	posthumous	prologue
palatable	pattern	photosynthesis	posture	prolong
palatial	pauper	phrase	potent	prolongation
palaver	peace	physical	potential	promenade
palette	peaceable	physician	poverty	prominent
palliates	peacock	physiotherapist	powder	promiscuous
palpable	peanuts	piano	practical	promise
palpitate	pearl	picketed	pragmatic	promissory
paltry	peculiar	picnic	prank	promote
pamphlet	pedagogy	picture	paraphernalia	promotion

panacea	peddle	picturesque	prawn	prompt
pandemic	pedigree	piece	precaution	promptly
pandemonium	pejorative	pierce	precede	promulgate
panegyric	penalty	pigeon	precedent	pronounce
panicky	pencil	pigment	precinct	pronunciation
panoply	penetrate	pillage	precious	propel
paper	penicillin	pinch	precipice	propeller
parable	penitence	pioneer	precipitous	property
parachute	penitentiary	pious	precision	prophecy
paradigm	pensive	pirouette	precocious	proposal
paradise	people	piteous	predecessor	propose
paradox	perambulate	pitiful	predicament	proprietary
paraffin	perceive	pivot	prefer	proprietor
paragon	perched	placate	preference	prosecute
paragraph	perennial	plagiarism	pregnant	proselyte
parallel	perforation	plagiarist	prejudice	prospectus
paralysis	performance	plague	preliminary	prosperous
paralyze	perfume	plaintiff	premeditate	prostrate
paramount	perilous	plausible	premier	protagonist
paranoia	perimeter	pleasant	premonition	protect
parapet	periodic	pleasure	preparation	prototype
paraphrase	periscope	plebeian	prerequisite	protraction
parasite	perjure	pledge	prerogative	protuberance
parcel	permanent	plenty	prescribe	proud
parch	permeate	plethora	present	proverb
pardon	permissible	pleurisy	preservative	provide
parent	permitted	plight	prestige	providence
parliament	pernicious	ploughed	prestigious	provinces
parochial	perpendicular	plumber	pretentious	provocation
parody	perpetrate	plumber	prevails	provoke
paroxysm	perplex	plumbing	prevalent	prowess
parquet	persecute	plummet	prevaricate	prudence
parrot	persevere	plump	previous	prudent
parsimonious	persistence	plunder	priest	pruning
parsley	person	plunge	primitive	psalm
partake	personify	pneumonia	principal	psyche
partial	persuade	pocket	printer	psychiatric
partiality	pertinence	poignancy	prison	psychic
participant	perturb	poignant	privilege	psychoanalyst
participation	perusal	point	probably	psychologist
particle	pervade	poise	probity	psychology

Vocabulary: The personal Dictionary

particular	perverse	poisonous	problem	publicly
partisan	pessimist	police	procedure	punctual
partition	pestilent	politician	proceed	pupil
partner	petrify	pollution	procession	purple
partnership	petticoat	polygamy	proclamation	purpose
passable	phantom	polyglot	procreation	pursuit
passion	Pharisee	polygon	prodigal	putative
passionate	pharmacy	polythene	product	puzzle
pastel	pharyngitis	pompous	profane	pyjamas
pastor	pharynx	popular	professional	Pythagoras
pastoral	phenomenal	population	proficiency	
patent	phenomenon	porridge	profile	

Q q is For Quebec*(Phonetic Alphabet)*

Words Beginning With The Letter Q

Three Letter Words

que

Four Letter Words

quad   quay   quid   quit   quiz

Words With More Letters

quack	quadrangle	quagmire	quarantine	queasy
qualify	quality	qualm	Quaker	quite
quarrel	quarrelsome	quarry	queer	quota
quash	quaver	queen	questionnaire	quantity
quench	question	quest	quicken	quake
queue	quibble	quick	quinoa	quarter
quickly	quiet	quirk	query	
quintet	quiver	quaint	queue	

Vocabulary: The personal Dictionary

R r is For Romeo *(Phonetic Alphabet)*

Words Beginning With The Letter <u>R</u>

Three Letter Words

rad	rag	ram	ran	rap	rat	raw	ray	red	rib	rid	rig	rim
rip	rob	rod	roe	rot	row	rub	rue	rug	rum	run	rut	rye

Four Letter Words

race	rack	raft	rage	raid	rail	rain	rake	ramp	rang
rank	rare	rash	rate	read	real	ream	reap	rear	reed
reel	rely	rent	rest	rice	rich	ride	rift	ring	riot
ripe	rise	risk	road	roam	roar	robe	rock	rode	role
roll	roof	room	root	rope	rose	rota	ruby	rude	rugs
ruin	rule	rush	rust						

Words With More Letters

rabbit	receive	relapse	reservation	revitalisation
rabble	recent	relative	reserve	revival
rabid	receptionist	release	reservoir	revocation
rabies	receptive	relegate	residence	revoke
racket	recess	relevant	residue	revolt
radiance	recession	reliance	resign	revolution
radiance	recipe	relic	resignation	revolve
radiant	recite	relief	resilience	rhetoric
radiate	reckless	religion	resistance	rhinoceros
radical	reckon	relinquish	resolute	rhizome
radio	recline	relocate	resolution	rhubarb
raggedy	recluse	reluctance	resolve	rhyme
railing	recognise	remain	resonant	rhythm
rainbow	recoil	remainder	resort	ribbon
rainforest	recollect	remarkable	resounding	ricochet
raise	recommence	remedial	resources	riddance
rally	recommend	remedy	respect	ridicule
ramble	recommendation	remember	respiration	ridiculous
rampage	reconcile	reminder	respite	riffraff
ramshackle	reconciliation	reminiscence	resplendent	right

rancour	reconnaissance	remission	respond	righteous
random	reconsider	remit	responsibility	rigid
range	reconstruct	remnant	restaurant	rigmarole
ransack	record	remorse	restitution	rigorous
rapacious	recover	remote	restoration	ringleader
rapid	rectify	remove	restore	rival
rapidity	recuperate	remunerate	restrain	rivalry
rapport	recur	renaissance	restrict	robbery
rapture	recurrent	render	result	robust
rapturous	redeem	rendezvous	resume	rocket
rascal	redolent	rendition	resumption	rollick
raspberry	redress	renegade	resurgence	roly-poly
ratification	reduce	renewal	resurrect	romance
ratify	redundant	renitence	resuscitate	romantic
ration	reeling	renounce	retail	rosemary
rationale	referee	renovate	retain	rotates
rattle	reference	renowned	retaliate	rotation
ravage	refine	renunciation	retard	rough
ravenous	reflect	reoccurrence	retardation	round
reach	reflex	repeal	reticence	rouse
reached	refract	repeat	retina	route
react	refrain	repellent	retinue	routine
reaction	refresh	repentant	retirement	rowdy
reactivate	refuge	repercussion	retort	royal
readiness	refugee	repetition	retouch	ruckus
ready	refulgent	rephrase	retract	rudiment
realise	refurbish	replica	retreat	rudimentary
realistic	refusal	replied	retrench	ruffian
reality	refuse	report	retribution	ruffle
realm	refute	repose	retrieval	rugged
reaping	regain	repository	return	rumble
reason	regal	reprehend	reunite	ruminates
reasonable	regatta	represent	revamp	rumour
reawaken	regime	repression	reveal	
rebate	region	reprimand	revel	
rebel	register	reprisal	revelation	
rebellious	regress	reprobate	revelry	
rebirth	regret	reproduce	revenge	
rebound	regular	reprove	reverberate	
rebuff	rehabilitate	reptile	revere	
rebuke	rehearsal	repugnant	reverend	

Vocabulary: The personal Dictionary

recall	reign	repulsion	reverential
recant	reigned	reputable	reversal
recap	reimburse	request	revert
recapitulate	reindeer	requires	review
recede	reinforce	requisite	revile
receipt	reiterate	resemble	revise
receivable	rejuvenate	resentment	revision

S s is For Sierra *(Phonetic Alphabet)*

Words Beginning With The Letter **S**

Three Letter Words

sad	sag	sap	sat	saw	sax	say	sea	see	set	sew	sex	she
shy	sim	sin	sip	sir	sis	sit	six	ski	sky	sly	sob	sod
son	sop	sow	soy	spa	spy	sty	sub	sue	sum	sun		

Four Letter Words

sack	safe	sail	sale	salt	same	sand	sane	save	scab
scam	scan	scar	seal	seam	sear	seat	sect	seed	seek
seem	seen	seer	self	sell	send	sewn	shed	shin	ship
shop	shot	show	shun	shut	sick	side	sift	sigh	sign
silk	silt	sing	sink	size	skin	skip	slab	slam	slap
slim	slip	slit	slot	slow	slug	snap	snip	snow	snug
soak	soap	soar	sock	sofa	soft	soil	sole	solo	some
song	soon	soot	sore	sort	soul	soup	sour	sown	span
spat	spin	spit	spot	stab	stag	star	stay	stem	step
stew	stir	stop	stud	such	suck	suit	sulk	sure	surf
swan	swap	swim							

Words With More Letters

sabotage	secretary	sneaker	stature	suffocate
saccharine	secular	snobbish	status	sugar
sacred	secure	sober	statute	suggest
sacrifice	sediment	sobriety	statutory	suicide
sacrilege	seduce	societal	staunch	suitable
sacrosanct	segment	sociology	stave	suitor
saddle	segregate	socks	steadfast	sullenness
sadness	seized	solemn	steal	summarise
safety	seizure	solitary	stealth	summer
saffron	seldom	solitude	steam	summon
sagacious	selection	solution	steep	sumptuous

Vocabulary: The personal Dictionary

sailor	selfless	something	steer	sundial
salient	senile	soothsay	stench	sundown
salivate	sensation	sophisticate	stereophonic	sunrise
salubrious	separate	sorcery	stereotype	sunset
salutation	sequel	sorrow	sterilization	super
salvage	sequence	sound	stigma	supercilious
salvation	sequential	source	stimulant	superficial
sample	sequin	southern	sting	superfluous
sanctify	serene	souvenir	stingy	superintendent
sanctimonious	serious	sovereign	stipulation	superiority
sanctuary	serpentine	spacious	stirrup	superlative
sanguine	servitude	spade	stitch	supersede
sanity	severe	spaghetti	stocky	supervision
sapient	shackle	spark	stodgy	supervisor
sarcasm	shadow	sparse	stomach	supplant
sarcastic	shall	speak	stone	supplement
satanic	shamble	species	stooge	supplementary
satellite	shard	specification	stool	supplication
satiate	shatter	specimen	stoop	support
satire	shenanigan	spectacle	stoppage	suppress
satisfy	shift	spectacular	storehouse	suppression
saturate	shifty	spectrum	storm	supreme
saucepan	shimmer	speechless	stormy	surface
saucer	shipwreck	speed	storyteller	surmise
savage	shirk	spend	straggle	surmount
savvy	shiver	spendthrift	straight	surpass
scaffold	shoal	sphere	strain	surplus
scald	shore	spherical	strange	surprise
scallop	shortcoming	sphinx	strategy	surrender
scalp	should	spice	strawberry	surreptitious
scandal	shoulder	spicy	streak	surrogate
scanty	shove	spinach	stream	surround
scapegoat	shrewd	spinster	streamer	surveillance
scared	shriek	spiral	streamlined	surveyor
scarf	shrine	spirit	street	susceptible
scarlet	shrink	spiritual	strength	suspect

scary	shrivel	spiteful	strenuous	suspend
scathe	shroud	splash	strict	suspension
scatter	shudder	splatter	strife	suspicious
scavenge	shuffle	spleen	strike	sustain
scenario	shuttle	splendour	string	sustenance
scene	siesta	split	stringent	swagger
scenery	significance	spoilt	strip	swarm
scenic	silence	sponge	stripe	sweat
scent	silhouette	sponsorship	stroll	sweep
sceptical	silver	spontaneity	strong	sweet
sceptre	similarity	spontaneous	structure	sweetener
schedule	simplicity	sporadic	stubborn	sweetheart
scheme	simulate	spouse	stubbornness	sweltering
scholar	simultaneous	sprain	studious	swerve
science	since	sprawl	stumble	swimmer
scientific	sincere	spread	stump	swindle
scientifically	singe	spree	stupendous	swipe
scientist	single	spring	stupid	switch
scintillating	singlet	sprint	stupor	swivel
scissors	singular	sprout	sturdy	sycamore
scoffed	sinister	sprouts	stutter	sycophant
scones	situation	spurn	style	syllable
scooter	skedaddle	squabble	suave	symbolic
scorch	skeleton	squalid	subdue	symmetrical
score	skyrocket	square	subject	sympathy
scorn	slate	squash	subjugate	symphony
scoundrel	slaughter	squat	sublime	symptom
scourge	sledge	squatter	submission	synagogue
scout	sleep	squawk	subordinate	syndicate
scrabble	sleeve	squeak	subpoena	synergy
scram	sleight	squeeze	subscribe	synonym
scrap	slender	squiggle	subsequent	synopsis
scratch	sleuth	squirm	subservient	synthetic
scrawl	slight	squirrel	subsidy	syringe
scream	sling	squirt	subsistence	syrup

Vocabulary: The personal Dictionary

screech	slithered	squishy	substantial	system
screen	sloppy	stable	substantive	
scribe	slothful	staccato	subterfuge	
scripture	sluggard	staggering	subterranean	
scrounge	sluggish	stagnation	subtle	
scrub	slumber	stalemate	subversion	
scruffy	smack	stamen	succeed	
scrumptious	smart	stamina	successfully	
scrunch	smear	standard	succession	
scythe	smirk	startle	succulent	
sealant	smooth	startling	succumb	
season	smoothie	state	sucker	
seaweed	smudge	statement	sudden	
seclude	snappy	station	suede	
secondary	snatch	statistics	suffering	
secret	sneak	statue	sufficient	

T t is For Tango *(Phonetic Alphabet)*

Words Beginning With The Letter **T**

Three Letter Words

tab	tad	tag	tan	tap	tar	tax	tea	tee	ten	the	tic	tie
tin	tip	toe	tom	ton	too	top	tot	tow	toy	try	tub	tug
tut	two											

Four Letter Words

tack	tact	tail	take	tale	talk	tall	tame	tank	tape
tart	task	taxi	teal	team	tear	tell	tend	tent	term
test	text	that	thaw	them	then	they	this	thou	thud
thug	tide	tidy	tier	tiff	tile	till	tilt	time	tint
tiny	tire	toad	toed	tofu	toga	toil	toll	tomb	tone
tore	tour	town	tram	trap	tray	trek	trim	trio	trip
trot	tsar	tuba	tube	tuft	tune	turf	turn	tusk	twig
twin	type								

Words With More Letters

tabby	tension	thrift	touch	trite
table	tentative	thrill	tough	triumph
tableau	tenuous	throat	tourist	triumphant
taboo	tepid	thrombosis	tournament	trivial
tabulation	terminal	throng	tourniquet	troop
taciturn	terminate	through	towards	trouble
tackle	terminology	thrust	towelling	troublesome
tactful	terminus	thumbnail	trace	trounce
taffeta	terrain	thump	tracksuit	troupe
tagliatelle	terrestrial	thunder	trade	trousers
tailor	terrific	thwart	trademark	trousseau
taint	terrifically	thyme	tradition	truce
talent	terrifying	ticket	traffic	trudge
tally	territorial	tickle	tragedy	truism

Vocabulary: The personal Dictionary

tamper	territory	timber	train	trump
tangent	terrorism	timid	traitor	truncate
tangerine	terrorist	tinsel	traitorous	truncheon
tangible	testament	tipsy	trample	trustee
tantalise	testify	tirade	tranquiliser	trustworthy
tantamount	testimonial	tissue	tranquillity	truth
tantrum	texture	titan	transaction	tuberculosis
tariff	thankful	titivate	transcend	Tuesday
tarnish	thaumaturgy	title	transfer	tuition
tarragon	theatre	tittle-tattle	transfiguration	tumble
taskmaster	theatrical	toast	transform	tumour
taste	theme	tobacconist	transformation	tumult
tatters	theoretical	toboggan	transgress	tumultuous
tattoo	theory	today	transparent	tunnel
taunt	therapeutic	toffee	transport	turbulence
taxation	therapy	together	transportation	tureen
teacher	thermometer	toilet	trauma	turquoise
teamwork	thespian	tolerable	travail	tussle
tease	Thessalonians	tolerance	travelled	tutelage
technique	thief	tomatoes	travesty	twaddle
tedious	thigh	tomorrow	trawler	twelfth
telepathy	thing	tongue	treacherous	twenty
telephone	think	tonic	tread	twiddle
telescope	thirsty	tonsillitis	treadmill	twilight
temper	thirteen	tonsils	treasure	twine
temperamental	thorn	topical	treasury	twinkle
temperature	thorough	topple	treatment	twist
temporal	thoroughbred	topsy-turvy	tremendous	twitch
tempt	thoroughfare	tornado	tremor	twitter
temptation	thought	torpedo	trend	tyranny
tenable	thoughtful	torpor	trepidation	tyrant
tenacious	thoughtless	torso	trial	
tendency	thrash	tortoise	tribe	
tender	thread	torturous	trick	
tenet	threat	total	trifle	
tense	threshold	totalitarian	trinket	

U u is For Umbrella *(Phonetic Alphabet)*

Words Beginning With The Letter U

Three Letter Words

ugh   ump   urn   use

Four Letter Words

ugly   undo   unit   unto   upon   urge   used   user

Words With More Letters

ubiquitous	unease	unnatural	unsatisfactory	upgrade
ulterior	unequivocal	unnecessary	unsavoury	upheaval
ultimate	unethical	unnerve	unscathed	uphold
ultimately	unfaithful	unobtrusive	unscrupulous	uppermost
umbrella	unfasten	unofficial	unseat	upright
umpire	unfit	unorthodox	unseemly	uproar
unacceptable	uniform	unpaid	unsettled	upset
unanimity	uniformity	unpalatable	unsightly	upsurge
unanimous	unimportant	unpleasant	unskilled	Uranus
unaware	union	unprecedented	unsound	urban
unbecoming	unique	unpretentious	unspeakable	urgency
unbelief	unison	unproductive	unstable	urgent
unbiased	unite	unqualified	unsurpassed	usage
unbind	unity	unravel	unswerving	useful
uncertain	universal	unrealistic	unsympathetic	useless
uncle	universality	unrefined	untrue	usher
unconscious	universe	unrelenting	untruth	usually
uncover	university	unrepentant	unusual	usurp
underage	unlawful	unresponsive	unveiling	utilise
undermine	unlearned	unrest	unwanted	utilitarian
underpants	unlikely	unrestricted	unwell	utility
underprivileged	unlucky	unrivalled	unwieldy	utmost
undersign	unmanageable	unroll	unwilling	utopian
understand	unmanly	unruffled	unwind	utter
undo	unmentionable	unruly	unwise	utterance
undulate	unmistakable	unsafe	upbeat	utterly

Vocabulary: The personal Dictionary

V v is For Victor *(Phonetic Alphabet)*

Words Beginning With The Letter V

Three Letter Words

van   vat   vee   vet   vex   via   vie   vow

Four Letter Words

vain	vary	vase	vast	veer	veil	vein	vend	vent	verb
very	vest	veto	vial	vibe	vice	view	vile	vine	void
vole	volt	vote							

Words With More Letters

vacant	vaporise	verge	vigour	vocalist
vacate	variable	verify	villain	vocation
vacation	variance	vermillion	villainous	vociferous
vaccinate	variation	versatile	vindicate	voice
vacillate	variegate	version	vindictive	volatile
vacuous	variety	vertical	vintage	volcano
vacuum	various	vertigo	violate	volition
vagabond	varnish	vesper	violence	volley
vagrant	vaticinator	vestige	violent	volume
vague	vault	vestment	violet	voluminous
vainglory	vector	veteran	virago	voluntary
valedictory	vehemence	veterinary	virgin	volunteer
valiant	vehement	vetoes	virile	voluptuous
valid	vehicle	viable	virtual	voracious
validate	velocity	vibrant	virtue	voracity
validity	veneer	vibration	virtuous	vouch
valley	venerable	vice versa	virulent	vowel
valour	vengeance	vicinity	virus	vulgar
valuable	venom	viciousness	viscose	vulgarism
valuation	venomous	vicissitude	visibility	vulnerable
value	ventilate	victim	visible	vying

vamoose	ventilation	victor	vision
vampire	ventilator	victorious	visit
vandalism	venture	victory	vital
vanilla	veracity	Vietnamese	vivacious
vanish	veranda	viewpoint	vivid
vanity	verbal	vigil	vixen
vanquished	verbatim	vigilance	vocabulary
vantage	verbose	vigorous	vocal

Vocabulary: The personal Dictionary

W w is For Whisky *(Phonetic Alphabet)*

Words Beginning With The Letter **W**

Three Letter Words

war was wax way web wed wee wen wet who why wig win
wit wiz woe wry

Four Letter Words

wade	waft	wage	waif	wail	wait	wake	walk	wall	wand
wane	want	ward	warm	warn	warp	wart	wary	wash	watt
wave	weak	weal	wear	weed	week	weep	weld	welt	well
were	wham	what	when	whim	whip	whom	wide	wife	wild
wile	will	wilt	wind	wine	wing	wink	wipe	wire	wise
wish	with	wolf	womb	wood	wool	word	work	worm	wrap
wren									

Words With More Letters

waffle	wayward	whiff	winter	worship
wafted	weakling	while	wisdom	worst
wager	weakness	whimper	wishy-washy	worth
waggle	wealth	whirl	wistful	worthless
waist	weariness	whisk	witch	worthy
waive	weary	whisper	witchcraft	wrack
waiver	weasel	whistle	withdraw	wrangle
wakeful	weather	whiting	withdrawal	wrapper
wallaby	weave	whole	wither	wrath
wallop	wedlock	wholehearted	without	wreak
wallow	Wednesday	wholesome	withstand	wreathe
waltz	weeping	wholly	wizard	wreck
wander	weigh	whoopee	wizardry	wreckage
wandering	weight	whoosh	woeful	wrench
warden	weird	whore	womankind	wrest
wardrobe	welcome	wickedness	wombat	wrestle
warfare	welfare	widespread	women	wretch

warped	wench	wield	wonder	wretchedness
warrant	wetland	wiggle	wonderful	wriggle
warranty	whack	wilderness	wonderment	wrinkle
warring	wharf	wilfulness	wondrous	wristwatch
waste	wheat	wiliness	wooden	write
wastefulness	wheel	wince	woolly	written
wasteland	wheeze	windiness	wordless	wrong
watchful	where	winner	worker	
watercress	wherewithal	winnow	worry	
waterish	whether	winsome	worse	

Vocabulary: The personal Dictionary

X x is For X-ray *(Phonetic Alphabet)*

Words Beginning With The Letter **X**

Four Letter Word

x-ray

Useful Words With More Letter

xylophone

Y y is For Yankee *(Phonetic Alphabet)*

Words Beginning With The Letter **Y**

Three Letter Words

yak   yam   yap   yaw   yay   yea   yen   yep   yes   yet   yew   yip
you   yum   yup

Four Letter Words

yank   yard   yarn   yawn   year   yell   yelp   yoga   yolk   your

Words With More Letters

yacht   yardstick   yawning   yearn   yeast
yelled   yellow   yesterday   yield   yoghurt
young   youngster   youthful   yummy

Z z is For Zulu *(Phonetic Alphabet)*

Words Beginning With The Letter **Z**

Three Letter Words

zag   zap   zed   zen   zig   zip   zit   zoo

Four Letter Words

zany   zeal   zero   zest   zone   zoom

Words With More Letters

zealous   zebra   zenith   zephyr   zigzag   zoology

ii.   Mnemonics

It is sometimes difficult to remember wow words when writing essays, especially during an examination so being prepared with relevant words will increase your chances of success. The purpose of this section is to demonstrate how to improve your writing skills by using mnemonic devices.

A mnemonic device helps the user to remember words, phrases or sentences. They are particularly useful when you have an order of words or a general list of words to remember. Below are some useful examples.

- ❖ How to remember the spelling of a word
  You can make up a sentence with the spelling of the word.

  Example: In order to remember how to spell, make up a sentence. In this example the commonly used sentence: '**B**ig **E**lephants **C**an **A**lways **A**dd **U**p **S**ums **E**asily' has been used to remember how to spell the word *'because'*. Popular mnemonics like this one adds fun to how one learns to spell new words.

- ❖ How to remember the elements of the use of language (AFOREST)

  AFOREST is a mnemonic that is used to remember the use of language in examinations. It stands for *alliteration, facts, opinions, repetition, emotive language, statistics,* and *the rule of three.* Below is a description of each word.

    o *Alliteration* refers to repetition of the same or similar initial consonant sounds in words that are close together. There is a list of alliteration at the back of this part of the book.

    o *Facts* are statements that can be proven. Identify the fact and back it up with evidence. References to impressions made and images provided in the text are two examples. Ensure that the information is presented in an orderly manner.

- *Opinions* are thoughts expressed by an individual and may not be proven. The writer's thoughts on the facts and opinions provided, the mood and tone of the text, the layout, and the persuasive techniques adopted should be expressed with clarity.

- *Repetition* is an effective strategy, especially when there is a balance between the frequency of the repetition, the intensity of the thought, and the variety in the tone of the message. Martin Luther King's "I Have a Dream" speech is a popular example.

- *Emotive language* is useful in engaging the reader and helps him or her relate to the hope, pain, or pleasure being expressed. When using emotive language, it is necessary to be clear what action the writer desires the reader or audience to take. It is essential for the writer to understand the emotional state that supports that action and use the appropriate words or expressions in the text. Emotional states include those that express anger, curiosity, confusion, inspiration, safety, and urgency. You can have a list of words for each type of emotion.

- *Statistics*: it is useful to include data and other statistics from credible sources to validate a point being presented.

- *The Rule of Three* is based on the understanding that people tend to remember three things. It is used to emphasise a point by providing supporting evidence. For example, Shakespeare's "Friends, Romans, countrymen…"

Vocabulary: The personal Dictionary

It is sometimes difficult to remember all the words you have learned when you are in the examination hall so it is helpful to have a reliable tool. Mnemonics that you have memorised and practised using several times before a composition test will not only help you succeed but will prove useful in life. Listed below are some more mnemonics you can use.

- ❖ Mnemonic for planning an essay or letter (SPLAT)
  SPLAT stands for Structure, Purpose, Language, Audience and Tone

    o Structure – Decide how the essay or letter should be presented.
        - The introduction
        - How many paragraphs and content of each paragraph so that the piece of writing is coherent.
    o Purpose - Be clear about the objective of the essay or letter
        - Why are you writing the letter?
        - What would you like to achieve or what change in thought or action would you like to see?
    o Language – Choose the appropriate words and terminologies (i.e. formal or informal words, biased, imagery, connectives or other parts of speech).
    o Audience – The recipient or reader
    o Tone – The impression and feeling you would like the reader to have or experience.
        - How will the recipient feel when reading the letter? How does it sound?
        - Does the piece of writing sound angry, understanding, opinionated, persuasive, objective, humorous?

- ❖ How to remember specific types of words

    o Example 1: Poetic devices
    There are so many poetic devices and remembering all of them can be challenging. You can make up a mnemonic

device to help you. Below is an example of a mnemonic to help learners remember fixed form poems.

The mnemonic is: *Brother Charles England Slowly Explained Harry's Long Life Sentence To Sally Sinclair Outside Pat's Shop In Valley Road.*

This mnemonic stands for: *Ballad, Concrete poetry, Epitaph, Spenserian sonnet, Epigram, Haiku, Limerick, Lyric, Sestina, Triolet, Sonnet, Shakespearian sonnet, Ode, Pantoum, Sonnet Sequence, Italian Sonnet, Villanelle, Rondeau.*

- **Example 2:** Order of adjectives in a sentence

    Listed below is the order of adjectives in a sentence.

    1. quantity/general opinion or **_n_**_umber_
    2. quality or specific _opinion_
    3. _size_
    4. _shape_
    5. _age_
    6. _colour_
    7. proper adjective (e.g. _nationality_, place of _origin_, or _material_)
    8. _purpose_ or qualifier

    The letters in bold and underlined above have been used to form the following sentence that will help you remember the order:

    No one saw Sister Ann's cousin, Natalie, make pancakes.

Vocabulary: The personal Dictionary

- Example **3:** Wow words for letter writing

    Choose a word with seven or more letters so that you can use it to remember words for a specific type of letter. In the example below, the word *'special'* has been used to remind a writer of the words relevant to a letter of application for employment. Each letter of the word *'special'* refers to a useful word for an application for work.

    *s*ubstantial
    *p*rofessional
    *e*fficient
    *c*onscientious
    *i*nsightful
    *a*nalytical
    *l*eader

- Example 4: Wow words for essay writing

    Below is a statement that can be used to remind you of some wow words. You can create words, phrases or sentences for specific purposes.

    Example 4A: Use of a sentence

    A student who correctly spells and appropriately includes a number of wow words in an essay will score highly in any tests. Making up a sentence is a way to remember such words. In the example below, a very long sentence is used to help students remember over thirty wow words in preparation for a test.

The long sentence:

Adam and David exercised in Paul's office during lunch, claiming that Michael, Charlie, Sarah, Jane, Richard and Peter opened the door for Valerie so they took the opportunity to get in very quickly.

Mnemonic device	Wow Word
Adam	authoritative
And	atrocious
David	despicable
Exercised	exasperate
In	infuriate
Paul's	pessimistic
Office	outrageous
During	disillusioned
Lunch	libellous
Claiming	contradict
That	tragic
Michael	manipulative
Charlie	controversial
Sarah	sarcastic
Jane	judgemental
Richard	reprimand
And	aggravate
Peter	placid
Opened	obnoxious
The	tolerance
Door	diabolical
For	forlorn
Valerie	vengeance
So	spiteful
They	twitching
Took	threatening
The	thriller
Opportunity	offensive
To	transparency
Get	gigantic
In	inconsiderate
Very	vigilance
Quickly	quintessential

Vocabulary: The personal Dictionary

You are required to use the same statement to make a list of some *positive* wow words in the table below. Some words have already been included:

Mnemonic Device	Wow Word
Adam	
And	
David	
Exercised	exceptional
In	
Paul's	proactive
Office	
During	
Lunch	
Claiming	
That	
Michael	
Charlie	
Sarah	
Jane	
Richard	reinvigorate
And	
Peter	
Opened	
The	
Door	
For	
Valerie	
So	
They	
Took	
The	
Opportunity	
To	
Get	
In	
Very	
Quickly	

Example 4B: Oxymoron

Use a sentence to remember oxymora, sentence openers or topic sentences and improve the quality of your essay. Below is an example of a sentence used to remember a list of oxymoron's:

Sentence: *During Christmas In Canada, Charlie Proposed To Christine, A Virtual Stranger.*

This stands for:

Deafening silence
Conventional wisdom
Industrial park
Constant change
Constructive criticism
Permanent change
Terribly nice
Conspicuous absence
Abundant poverty
Virtual reality
Strangely familiar

Refer to a list of oxymoron's at the end of this section for more examples. You can also use the template in Appendix 11 to create a mnemonic.

Example 4C: Lyrics of a song

Use the lyrics of a song you like or a popular one that you know to remember some wow words. In the table below, the lyrics of the song ' *Somewhere over the rainbow'* has been used as a mnemonic for positive and negative words.

You are required to complete the table with some wow words of your choice. Some of the words in the alphabetical lists of words in Part 1 may be included.

Vocabulary: The personal Dictionary

Mnemonic (Lyrics)	Wow Word (Positive)	Wow Words (Negative)
Somewhere		
over		
the		
rainbow		
way		
up		
high		
there's		
a		
land		
that		
I		
heard		
of		
once		
in		
a		
lullaby		

Use the template in Appendix 11 to create a mnemonic using the lyrics of another song.

Example 4D: Letters of the Alphabet

The letters of the alphabet can also be used to remember wow words; just as children use them to remember their first words. Below is an alphabetical list of words. Learn these or complete the last grid with some wow words of your choice. Use the template in Appendix 11 to create other lists of words for specific purposes.

Mnemonic	Wow Word (Positive)	Wow Words (Negative)
A	ambidextrous	awkward
B	brilliance	boredom
C	communication	cantankerous
D	debonair	disdainful
E	enchanting	embarrassment
F	fabulous	frightened
G	graceful	ghastly
H	hilarious	haunt
I	impartial	inferior
J	jubilation	jealous
K	kindness	kidnap
L	laughter	lonesome
M	magnificence	melancholy
N	natural	nuisance
O	obedient	obnoxious
P	picturesque	pessimistic
Q	quaint	quarrelsome
R	radiant	ridiculous
S	sophisticated	scalding
T	thoughtful	terrible
U	universal	unbelievable
V	victorious	venomous
W	wonderful	worry
Y	youthful	yell
Z	zealous	zombie

Vocabulary: The personal Dictionary

Fill the table below with your words

Mnemonic	Wow Word (Positive)	Wow Words (Negative)
A		
B		
C		
D		
E		
F		
G		
H		
I		
J		
K		
L		
M		
N		
O		
P		
Q		
R		
S		
T		
U		
V		
W		
X		
Y		
Z		

List of Alliterations

back burner (put...on the)	a bee in your bonnet	a labour of love
a pig in a poke	a way with words	all that glitters is not gold
as good as gold	back breaker	back to basics
back-biting	bad blood	bare bones
bated breath	bear the brunt of	best buddies
beat around the bush	belle of the ball	best and brightest
best buy	bet your bottom dollar	better safe than sorry
big bang theory	big brother	big bucks
bigger and better	birthday boy	bite the bullet
blind as a bat	blood brother	boom to bus
bottom of the barrel	bounce back	bread and butter
bright-eyed and bushy-tailed	building blocks	busy as a bee
by the book	cash crop	chit-chat
class clown	clear cut	close call
code of conduct	common cold	common courtesy
cool as a cucumber	cream of the crop	creepy crawlies
crystal clear daredevil	daydream	dead as a doornail
dead duck	do or die	down in the dumps
drip dry	dry as dust	dull as dishwater
epic elephants	eat edible eggs	fact finding
fall head over heels	fan the flames	fancy footwork
fast and furious	father figure	fear factor
feast or famine	feeding frenzy	few and far between
fickle finger of fate	fight or flight	fond farewell
forgive and forget	frequent flier	from the frying pan to the fire
gas guzzler	gentle giant	gift of the gab
give up the ghost go for the gold	good as gold	hale and hearty
half-hearted	have a heart	heaven and hell
heavy hitter	high hopes	hit the hay
home sweet home	house and home	insult to injury
it takes two to tango	Jack and Jill	jump for joy
larger than life	last laugh	law of the land
leave/left in the lurch	like it or lump it	live and learn
melt in your mouth	method to the madness	mind over matter
moaning Minnie	motormouth	move mountains
naughty or nice	neck and neck	new lease on life
no love lost	not on your nelly	now or never
out of order	part and parcel	party pooper
peas in a pod	peer pressure	pen pal
penny wise and pound foolish	Peter Piper picked a peck	of pickled peppers
pinch pennies	practice makes perfect	prim and proper
Primrose path	proper planning prevents	poor performance
pull any punches	rags to riches	rant and rave
rave reviews	right as rain	Russian roulette
safe and sound	secret sauce	shape up or ship out
shell-shocked	ship shape	sink or swim
slippery slope	slowly but surely	smooth sailing
sorry sight	spending spree	spoil sport

Vocabulary: The personal Dictionary

star struck	stars and stripes	sweet sixteen
temper tantrum	the grass is greener	the lap of luxury
the more the merrier	think tank	through thick and thin
time and tide	tip toe	tip top
tongue tied	tongue twisters	tools of the trade
treasure trove	trials and tribulations	vice versa
waste not, want not	weeping willow	
what's good for the goose is good for the gander		
where the rubber meets the road		
where there's a will, there's a way	whistle while you work	whole-hearted
wishy-washy	wonders of the world	words of wisdom
yin and yang	zig-zag	

List of Oxymora

- above ground
- altogether separate
- apparently invisible
- barely dressed
- blind spot
- cheap jewellery
- climb down
- conspicuous absence
- conventional wisdom
- critical praise
- deafening silence
- doing nothing
- easy task
- even odds
- fairly nasty
- few more
- firm handshake
- free trade
- funny business
- good grief
- guest host
- holy war
- hot ice
- industrial park
- irate patient
- large minority
- living fossil
- loosely packed
- mighty weak
- modern history
- narrow range
- nature preserve
- nothing much
- objective opinion
- oddly familiar
- once again
- only choice
- original copy
- paper tablecloth
- passive resistance
- pretty ugly
- quite unlikely
- recorded live
- retired worker
- same difference
- short distance
- slumber party
- still life
- all alone
- another one
- assistant principal
- behave badly
- calm breeze
- civil war
- cold sweat
- constant change
- crash landing
- crowded room
- defensive attack
- dotted line
- escaped prisoner
- extensive briefing
- farewell reception
- final draft
- forgotten memories
- fresh frozen
- genuine imitation
- ground up
- half empty
- home office
- ill health
- inside out
- job hunting
- lead balloon
- long briefs
- loyal opposition
- minor disaster
- muted sound
- nasty fine
- neutral colour
- now then
- obstructed view
- old boy
- one another
- open bar
- outer core
- park drive
- permanent change
- primitive technology
- random order
- relative stranger
- sad clown
- second best
- silent alarm
- sports scholarship
- strange friend
- almost exactly
- anxious patient
- awfully good
- big baby
- cardinal sin
- clearly confused
- come away
- constructive criticism
- criminal justice
- cruel joke
- divorce court
- down escalator
- essentially useless
- extinct life
- feeling numb
- finally begun
- foreign national
- front end
- global village
- growing smaller
- hard water
- homeless shelter
- income tax
- invisible ink
- jumbo shrimp
- live recording
- loose tights
- mandatory option
- mobile home
- mutually exclusive
- natural actor
- never again
- numb feeling
- occupied space
- old news
- one pair
- open secret
- paid volunteer
- partially completed
- personal business
- questionable answer
- real potential
- restless sleep
- safety hazard
- serious play
- sit up
- stand down
- strangely familiar

Vocabulary: The personal Dictionary

student teacher	studio apartment	terribly nice
top floor	tragic comedy	travel lodge
true story	uninvited guest	unknown identity
unsung hero	unusual routine	utter silence
very little	virtual reality	war games
well-known secret	white chocolate	young adult

PART2

General Knowledge Questions

Lack of information cannot be used as an excuse for not furthering your knowledge. Every city has a public library full of appropriate books, no matter what your area of interest.- Catherine Pulsifer

Vocabulary: The personal Dictionary

Introduction

People who have a good general knowledge of the world are often regarded as intelligent. The British Broadcasting Corporation's (BBC) popular show, Mastermind, celebrates those who know these facts. Candidates are often asked general knowledge questions when invited for an interview so the more informed an applicant is, the better their chances of success. Sources of general knowledge include: the news, documentaries, newspapers, textbooks, encyclopaedias, and periodicals. Participating in debates, quizzes, and doing crosswords are also useful activities.

i.   Practice Questions

Below are over two hundred and fifty general knowledge questions for you to attempt. All the answers to the questions in each alphabetical set start with the letter of that group. The answers to all the questions are at the end of this part of the book.

1. What is the name of the mountain system of north-west Africa that stretches from the Atlantic Ocean through Morocco, Algeria and Tunisia? _____
2. Which river carries the maximum amount of water into the sea? _____
3. What is the scientific name for vitamin C? _____
4. What is the name of the only continent occupied by one nation? _____

5. What is the name of the smallest county in Northern Ireland? _____

6. What is the Spanish word for 'armed forces'? _____

7. What is the name of a small edentate mammal found in Central and South America? _____

8. What is the name of a chemical element in the periodic system with the symbol *As*? _____

9. What is the name given to the act of maliciously setting fire to a building? _____

10. What is the name given to the study of celestial bodies, their positions and motions in the sky? _____

11. What is the name of the largest state in the USA? _____

12. What is the name of the fruit that contains the most protein? _____

B

1. What is the name of the capital city of Mali? _____

2. What is the name of small cargo vessel, flat-bottomed and used in rivers, canals and coastal waters? _____

3. What is the name of the chemical element with the symbol *Ba*? _____

Vocabulary: The personal Dictionary

4. What is the name of a herbaceous plant consumed by humans and livestock? _____
5. What is the name of an instrument used to measure atmospheric pressure? _____
6. What is the name of the liquid produced by the cells in the liver? _____
7. Which bird is the international symbol of happiness? _____
8. What is the name of the founder of modern Germany? _____
9. What is the French term, now used in English to describe a way of life characterized by living from day to day? _____
10. What is the name of the inland state in South America whose neighbours are Brazil, Peru, Paraguay, Argentina and Chile? _____
11. Who invented the television? _____
12. Who invented the vacuum cleaner? _____

C

1. What is the art of beautiful hand writing that adheres to certain defined aesthetics canons? _____
2. The Gulf of Sian lies to the south-west of this country. What is its name? _____

3. What is the method of concealment that was developed by the military? _____
4. What is the capital of Venezuela? _____
5. What is a community of ants called? _____
6. What is a baby swan called? _____
7. What is the name of the fastest mammal on earth? _____
8. In which war was the charge of the Light Brigade? _____
9. Which country grew the first orange? _____
10. In the Chinese calendar, what year follows the year of the Monkey? _____
11. What disease did Tchaikovsky die from? _____

D

1. What is the literal translation of the word Bedouin? _____
2. What name is given to: the state of finding it hard to get out of the bed in the morning? _____
3. What is the name of the Hindu festival that is known as 'the festival of light'? _____
4. What is the name of the first credit card? _____
5. Which country did the USA buy the Virgin islands from?

Vocabulary: The personal Dictionary

_____

6. Which leader lives in The Potala Palace? _____

7. What type of animal is a Samoyed? _____

8. What does a drosomoter measure? _____

9. What colour is cerulean? _____

10. What is biltong? _____

11. Nekal was the first type of what product? _____

12. What is the common name of the Lent Lily? _____

13. If you were crapulous what would you be? _____

14. What river flows through eight countries and four capital cities? _____

15. What is the national flower of Mexico? _____

16. A paddling is a group of which animals? _____

17. What is dittology? _____

18. Which insect has the best eyesight? _____

19. Who invented the light bulb? _____

E

1. In which country did draughts (checkers) originate?
   _____

2. What ingredient must French ice cream contain by law?
   _____

3. What Italian habit did Thomas Coyrat introduce to England 1608? _____

4. In which country is the port of Alexandria? _____

5. In which country did the first industrial revolution take place?
   _____

6. Which part of the human body has the thinnest skin?
   _____

F

1. Where could you spend a Markka? _____

2. What are lentigines? _____

3. Where is the world's largest aquarium? _____

4. How many chambers does the human heart have?
   _____

Vocabulary: The personal Dictionary

5. How many lines are there in a Limerick? _____

6. Ictheologists study what? _____

7. What is ikebana? _____

8. Which bird turns it head upside down to eat? _____

9. Translated literally, what does television mean? _____

G

1. Excluding religious works what is the world's top selling book? _____

2. What colour is the gemstone, Peridot? _____

3. What does the name Tabitha mean? _____

4. If you have Chlorosis, what colour does the skin go? _____

5. In which country did the turnip originate? _____

6. Who was the first man in space? _____

7. What country is nearest to the North Pole? _____

8. The length of what is approximately one-tenth, the circumference of earth? _____

9. Which country was known as the Gold Coast? _____

10. The Pindus is the main mountain range in what country? _____

11. Skordalia is the name of a dish from which country? _____

12. What animal's name, when translated from Arabic means 'He who walks fast'? _____

H

1. What is the horn of a rhinoceros made from? _____

2. What is the most common element on earth? _____

3. Who invented the safety pin? _____

4. Which song is sung the most in the world? _____

5. What is the literal meaning of the word, The Acropolis?

Vocabulary: The personal Dictionary

_____

6. Which city hosted the 1952 Olympics? _____

7. The young of what animal is called an Eyas?
_____

I

1. What does an entomologist study? _____

2. In which country is Mount Vesuvius? _____

3. What links Goa, Kerula, Assam and Bihar?
_____

4. In business, what does the abbreviation IMF mean?
_____

5. What were the first false teeth made from?
_____

6. Fredrick Sanger discovered which medical life saver?
_____

7. Trypanophobia is fear of what? _____

8. Calico cloth was invented in which country?
_____

J

1. Which country is known as the land of the rising sun? _____

2. What are Kreplach? _____

3. Who was eaten by dogs in the Old Testament? _____

4. What is the first name of Professor Moriaties? _____

5. Which country first started using Venetian Blinds? _____

6. Which organization was founded by Ignatius Loyola? _____

7. In which country are days known as Fire day, Water day and Wood day? _____

K

1. In the late 1950s and early 1960s, The Mau Mau were regarded as terrorists in which country? _____
2. What is the correct name for a baby otter? _____
3. What is the highest mountain in Africa? _____

Vocabulary: The personal Dictionary

4. What is another name for seaweed? _____
5. Where on the body is the patella? _____
6. Who invented the washing machine? _____

L

1. What is the world's most popular green vegetable? _____

2. Which African country was founded by Americans? _____

3. What is the name of the longest river in France? _____

4. Which city has the longest metro system? _____
5. What is the name of the national flower of Italy? _____

6. What is the capital of Peru? _____

M

1. What is the Roman Numeral for 1000? _____

2. What is the name of one of the three most spoken languages in the world? _____

3. What is the name of the main ailment that the drug called Quinine cures? _____

4. What is the name of the capital city of the Philippines?
   _____

5. What name is given to the galaxy that contains our solar system? _____

6. What leaf appears on the national flag of Canada?
   _____

7. Which German city hosted the 1972 Olympics?
   _____

8. Which comic book company shares its name with a word meaning 'to look at with awe'? _____

9. In mathematics, what name is giving to the most common value in a set of data? _____

10. What is the name of the young boy raised by wolves in Kipling's 'The Jungle Book'? _____

11. Whose autobiography was called 'The long walk to Freedom'?
    _____

N

1. What sugary fluid, found in plants, is collected by bees to make honey? _____

Vocabulary: The personal Dictionary

2. Which country moved its capital from Lagos to Abuja in 1991?
   _____

3. What is the outermost planet of our solar system?
   _____

4. What is the positive square root of 81? _____

5. Which chemist, famous for a series of prizes named after him, invented dynamite? _____

6. In Greek mythology, which youth fell in love with his own reflection? _____

7. Who sold Louisiana to the USA in 1803? _____

8. How many zeros are there in a billion? _____ N

9. The spice called Mace is made from what nut?
   _____

10. Where is the home of the prime meridian? _____

11. Triskadeccaphobia is the fear of what? _____

O

1. What is the capital city of Canada? _____

2. What city is home to England's oldest university?
   _____

3. What name is given to a polygon with eight straight sides? _____

4. What is the 24th and last letter of the Greek alphabet? _____

5. What chemical element has atomic number 8? _____

6. What name is given to a figure of self-contradictory speech, such as 'deafening silence' or 'living dead'? _____

7. Citius Altius Fortius is the motto of what organization? _____

8. What is the main ingredient of sauce Lyonnaise? _____

P

1. Which city was destroyed when Mount Vesuvius erupted in 79 A.D.? _____

2. Which fruit gets its name from the Latin for 'seeded apple'? _____

3. 'All children, except one, grow up' is the first line of what classic children's novel? _____

Vocabulary: The personal Dictionary

4. Rockhopper is the name given to which species of which bird?
   _____

5. Who became President of Russia for the second time in May 2012? _____

6. 2, 3, 5, 7 and 11 are the first five of what sequence of numbers? _____

7. What ocean goes to the deepest depths? _____

8. What is the currency of Chile? _____

9. What does the chemical symbol K stand for?
   _____

10. What planet did Clyde Tombaugh discover in 1930?
    _____

11. What is the groove located just below the nose and above the middle of the lips called? _____

12. What bird is the symbol of Penguin books (children's section)?
    _____

13. What is the capital of Sicily? _____

14. What is the longest river in Italy? _____

Q

1. Which mathematical term describes "half of a half"? _____

2. From the Italian for '40 days', what name is given to an isolation period for people or animals with a contagious disease? _____

3. Due to its consistency and colour, how is the element mercury commonly known? _____

4. What is the capital of Ecuador? _____

5. What writing implement was made from the feather of a large bird? _____

6. In Victor Hugo's novel, what is the name of 'The Hunchback of Notre Dame'? _____

7. Brisbane is the state capital of which South East Australian state? _____

8. Samuel de Champlain founded which city? _____

R

1. What is the Islamic equal to the red cross? _____
2. An unkindness is a group of what birds? _____
3. Which Hungarian inventor is famous for a cube puzzle he invented in 1974? _____

Vocabulary: The personal Dictionary

4. Often called a diamond, what shape has four equal sides and two pairs of equal angles? _____
5. What fruit is the basis of a melba sauce? _____
6. What disease, a softening of the bones, is caused by a deficiency of vitamin D? _____
7. What is the main unit of currency in India? _____
8. In the Christmas song, what is the name of the 'red-nosed reindeer'? _____
9. What are you supposed to give/get for 40 years of marriage? _____
10. What is the other name for German measles? _____
11. What is the capital city of Morocco? _____

S

1. In golf what name is given to the No 3 wood? _____
2. What type of acid is used in car batteries? _____
3. What is the commonest symbol on flags of the world? _____
4. In 1829, what common item did Walter Hunt invent? _____
5. What animal lives in a drey? _____

6. What did God create on the fifth day (both)?
   _____

7. Which European country is divided into areas called Cantons?
   _____

8. 'Basking', 'Mako' and 'Thresher' are all species of what animal? _____

9. The is the name of a famous Disney character that means lion in Swahili. What is it? _____

10. What is the medical name for the shoulder blade?
    _____

11. A lion holding a sword appears on the flag of what country?
    _____

12. Guru Nanak was the founder of what religion?
    _____

13. In 1796, Edward Jenner developed the first successful vaccine against what disease? _____

14. What is the currency in Israel? _____

15. What is rum made from? _____

16. Who invented the train? _____

T

1. What Italian building material translates as baked earth?
   _____

2. Which medical tool was developed by Sanctorius in 1612?
   _____

Vocabulary: The personal Dictionary

3. What was discovered in 1922 by Howard Carter? _____

4. What did William Addis invent in prison? _____

5. Sn is the chemical symbol for what element? _____

6. Henry VII was the first monarch of which British royal house? _____

7. 'Score' is an old-fashioned term for what number? _____

8. What branch of mathematics deals with the relation between the sides and angles of triangles? _____

9. What island forms a country with Trinidad? _____

10. Which magazine annually publishes an issue called 'Person of the Year'? _____

11. What is the national flower of Australia? _____

12. What is the name of the place known as the roof of the world? _____

13. What is the name of the largest wildcat? _____

U

1. What legendary animal resembles a horse with a single horn growing from its forehead? _____

2. What object did William Herschel discover on March 13,

1781? _____

3. From 1971 to 1979, Idi Amin was President of what country? _____

4. What does the letter 'U' stand for in the abbreviation U.F.O.? _____

5. What type of light, found in sunlight, has a wavelength shorter than visible light but longer than X-rays? _____

6. Pakistan has two official languages: English and which other? _____

7. Which annual sporting event between two teams started in 1829? _____

V

1. What is the name is diluted acetic acid more commonly known? _____

2. From the French word for 'bicycle', what name is given to a purpose-built cycling arena? _____

3. What name is given to the professional NFL team based in Minneapolis, Minnesota? _____

4. What name is given to a female fox? _____

Vocabulary: The personal Dictionary

5. 'Spike', 'Block' and 'Dig' are terms used in what sport?
   _____

6. Which award has the words for valour on it?
   _____

7. What is the name of the coldest place on earth?
   _____

8. What is the name of the place known as the city of canals?
   _____

W

1. In 1903, which brothers made the first controlled powered air-flight?_____

2. Which Scottish scientist gives his name to the S.I. unit of power?_____

3. Eeyore, Piglet and Christopher Robin are friends of which fictional bear?_____

4. Which animated character is the owner of dog Gromit?_____

5. At what 1815 battle was Napoleon Bonaparte defeated?_____

6. The All England Club hosts which annual Grand Slam tennis

tournament?_____

7. What is measured on the Beaufort scale? _____

8. Who is the only American president elected unopposed? _____

X

1. What is the name of a chemical element, present in air and number 54 in the periodic table? _____

2. What musical instrument gets its name from the Greek words for 'wood' and 'sound'? _____

3. What plant tissue transports water and dissolved nutrients upwards from the root? _____

4. Since 2008, what name have Sony given to their range of smartphones and tablets? _____

5. Cyclops, Iceman and Wolverine are members of what superhero group? _____

6. Wilhelm Röntgen won the 1901 Nobel Prize for Physics for his discovery of what? _____

Vocabulary: The personal Dictionary

1. What was Hebe the goddess of? _____

2. Which Chinese river is known as the Chang Jiang in its own language? _____

3. What imperial unit of measurement is equal to 0.9144 metres? _____

4. A type of what microscopic fungus is used to make bread dough rise? _____

5. The words 'bagel', 'golem' and 'schnozzle' all derive from what language? _____

6. What is the name of the dark force that opposes 'yang' in traditional Chinese philosophy? _____

7. Sana'a is the capital of what country? _____

8. What is the name of the skullcap worn by Jewish males at prayer or on some ceremonial occasions? _____

9. What is the westernmost and smallest of Canada's three federal territories bordering Alaska? _____

Z

1. What country is known as the Land of Copper?
   _____

2. The Victoria Falls can be found on which river?
   _____

3. What is the name of the largest island in Denmark? _____

4. What was Poland's currency before the Euro?
   _____

5. What metal is used to galvanise steel? _____

6. Which German Count has a mode of transportation named after him? ? _____

7. What road sign was first introduced to the United Kingdom on 31 October 1951? _____

8. What element does the chemical symbol Zr, represent? _____

9. What is the name of the last King of Albania?
   _____

10. What is the name for slender green Italian marrows?
    _____

11. What digit does not exist in Roman Numerals?
    _____

Vocabulary: The personal Dictionary

ii.   Answers To General Knowledge Questions

A
1. Atlas Mountains 2. The Amazon River
3. Ascorbic Acid 4. Australia 5. Armagh 6. Armada 7. Armadillo
8. Arsenic 9. Arson 10. Astronomy 11. Alaska 12. Avocado

B
1. Bamako 2. Barge 3. Barium 4. Barley 5. Barometer
6. Bile 7. Bluebird 8. Bismarck 9. Bohemian 10. Bolivia
11. (John Logie) Baird 12. (Hubert) Booth

C
1. Calligraphy 2. Cambodia 3. Camouflage 4. Caracas 5. Colony
6. Cygnet 7. Cheetah 8. Crimean 9. China 10. Chicken
11. Cholera

D
1. Desert dweller 2. Dysania 3. Diwali 4. Diners Club 5. Denmark
6. Dalai Lama 7. Dog 8. Dew 9. Deep blue 10. Dried meat
11. Detergent 12. Daffodil 13. Drunk 14. Danube 15. Dahlia
16. Ducks 17. Double meaning 18. Dragonfly 19.(Humphrey) Davy

E
1. Egypt 2. Eggs 3. Eating with forks 4. Egypt 5. England
6. Eye

F
1. Finland 2. Freckles 3. Florida (Epcot Centre) 4. Four 5. Five
6. Fish 7. Flower arranging 8. Flamingo 9. Far seeing

G

1. Guinness Book Of Records
2. Green
3. Gazelle
4. Green
5. Greece
6. (Yuri) Gagarin
7. Greenland
8. Great wall of China
9. Ghana
10. Greece
11. Greece
12. Giraffe (From Xirapha)

H

1. Hair
2. Hydrogen
3. (Walter) Hunt
4. Happy Birthday
5. Highest Point (in a city)
6. Helsinki
7. Hawk

I

1. Insects
2. Italy
3. India
4. International Monetary Fund
5. Ivory
6. Insulin
7. Injections
8. India

J

1. Japan
2. Jewish Ravioli
3. Jezebel
4.
5. Japan
6. Jesuits
7. Japan (Tuesday, Wednesday and Thursday)

K

1. Kenya
2. Kitten
3. Kilimanjaro
4. Kelp
5. Knee
6. (James) King

L

1. Lettuce
2. Liberia
3. Loire
4. London
5. Lily
6. Lima

M

1. M
2. Mandarin
3. Malaria
4. Manila
5. Milky Way
6. Maple
7. Munich
8. Marvel
9. Mode
10. Mowgli
11. Nelson Mandela

Vocabulary: The personal Dictionary

N

1. Nectar 2. Nigeria 3. Neptune 4. Nine 5. (Alfred) Nobel
6. Narcissus 7. Napoleon 8. Nine 9. Nutmeg
10. National Maritime Museum, Greenwich 11. Number

O

1. Ottawa 2. Oxford 3. Octagon 4. Omega 5. Oxygen
6. Oxymoron 7. Olympics 8. Onion

P

1. Pompeii 2. Pomegranate 3. Peter Pan 4. Penguin 5. (Vladimir) Putin
6. Prime numbers 7. Pacific Ocean 8. Peso 9. Potassium 10. Pluto
11. Philtrum 12. Puffin 13. Palermo 14. Po

Q

1. Quarter 2. Quarantine 3. Quicksilver 4. Quito 5. Quill
6. Quasimodo 7. Queensland 8. Quebec

R

1. Red Crescent 2. Raven 3. (Erno) Rubik 4. Rhombus 5. Raspberries
6. Ricketts 7. Rupee 8. Rudolph 9. Ruby 10. Rubella
11. Rabat

S

1. Spoon 2. Sulphur 3. Star 4. Safety Pin 5. Squirrel
6. Sea creatures and birds 7. Switzerland 8. Shark 9. Simba 10. Scapula
11. Sri Lanka 12. Sri Sikhism 13. Small Pox 14. Shekel 15. Sugar Cane
16. (George) Stevenson in 1821

T

1. Terracotta   2. Thermometer   3. Tutankhamen Tomb   4. Toothbrush   5. Tin
6. Tudor   7. Twenty   8. Trigonometry   9. Tobago   10. Time Magazine
11. The Wattle Blossom   12. Tibet   13. Tiger   14. The Wright Brothers

U

1. Unicorn   2. Uranus   3. Uganda   4. Unidentified   5. Ultraviolet
6. Urdu   7. University Boat Race (The)

V

1. Vinegar   2. Velodrome   3. Vikings   4. Vixen   5. Volleyball
6. Victoria Cross   7. Verkoyansk in Siberia   8. Venice

W

1. Wrights Brothers (The)   2. (James) Watt   3. Winnie The Pooh   4. Wallace
5. Waterloo   6. Wimbledon   7. Wind   8. (George) Washington

X

1. Xenon   2. Xylophone   3. Xylem   4. Xperia   5. X-men
6. X-rays

Y

1. Youth   2. Yangtze River   3. A Yard   4. Yeast   5. Yiddish
6. Yin   7. Yemen   8. Yamulka   9. Yukon

Z

1. Zambia   2. Zambezi   3. Zealand   4. Zloty   5. Zinc
6. Count Von Zeppelin   7. Zebra Crossing   8. Zirconium   9. Zog
10. Zucchini   11. Zero

PART 3

Vocabulary - Worksheets

Energy and persistence conquer all things.
- Benjamin Franklin

Introduction

In this part you will learn specific words relating to different aspects of life. The words are presented alphabetically and include: the names of animal, types of clothing, external parts of the body, financial terms, names of fruits, parts of an animals, parts of a bird, places, religions of the world, names of things found in a house, names of vegetables and types of games and sports. This part also includes lists of words related to art, architectural studies, cookery, electrical engineering, finance, geography, history, medical studies, science and sewing. You are required to learn the words and the appendices at the back of the book are useful resources to support your learning.

Vocabulary: The personal Dictionary

i. Names of animals

antelope
bear
caterpillar
dolphin
elephant
frog
giraffe
hippopotamus
iguana
jellyfish
kangaroo
llama
monkey
nightingale
ostrich
penguin
quail
rabbit
snake
tiger
urchin
vulture
whale
x-ray fish
yak
zebra

ii Architecture

arch	atrium	baluster	bay
cincture	cupola	curvilinear	eaves
fanlight	gable	hierarchy	jamb
joist	keystone	label	lacunar
lintel	moulding	oculus	parapet
pier	pinnacle	pitch	porch
portico	quoin	rotunda	sash
shed	spindle	studs	undercoat
ventilation	volute	wing	

Write more words below:

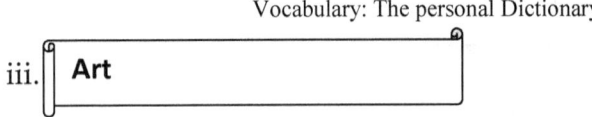

iii. Art

abstract	art nouveau	baroque	batik
byzantine	cameo	collage	cubism
diptych	engraving	etching	fresco
futurism	glyptic	grotesque	impasto
kinetic art	lithography	marquetry	mosaic
mural	naturalism	pop art	pastel
pop art	renaissance	stencil	surrealism
symbolism	tempera	water-colour	
woodcut	zincograph		

Write more words below:

iv. Types of clothing

- anorak
- blouse
- cardigan
- dress
- earrings
- flip-flop
- gloves
- hat
- ivy league sweater
- jumper
- kilt
- leggings
- mittens
- nightdress
- overcoat
- pyjamas
- quarter strap shoes
- raincoat
- scarf
- trousers
- underwear
- vest
- wellington boots
- x-ray glasses
- yoke
- zip

v. **Cookery**

agar	barbecue	baste	blanch
braise	caramelize	carve	crush
dice	dredge	drizzle	emulsify
fillet	flake	frost	garnish
non-stick	parboil	pinch	precook
reconstitute	roux	role	sauté
score	shuck	skewer	skim
gelatine	giblets	grate	Hor d'oeuvre
ice	jelly	knead	marinade
steam	toast	vinegar	whip
wonton	yeast	zest	

Write more words below:

vi. Electrical terms

- aluminium
- bandwidth
- cable
- duct
- Ethernet
- Fuse
- galvanise
- horsepower
- joule
- kilowatt
- limiter
- magnetic field
- n conductor cable
- oxidation
- plug
- quad-rated wire
- receptacle
- shunt
- terminal
- untested
- voltage
- weather proof
- XModem
- y- tape
- zero (balance)

Vocabulary: The personal Dictionary

vii. Everyday things

account	_____	_____
button	_____	_____
chair	_____	_____
drill	_____	_____
easel	_____	_____
foam	_____	_____
grinder	_____	_____
hair	_____	_____
inn	_____	_____
jotter	_____	_____
kettle	_____	_____
linen	_____	_____
mansion	_____	_____
nest	_____	_____
ornament	_____	_____
paint	_____	_____
quilt	_____	_____
rota	_____	_____
sewing machine	_____	_____
table	_____	_____
union jack	_____	_____
vale	_____	_____
wool	_____	_____
xylophone	_____	_____
yarn	_____	_____
zinc	_____	_____

viii.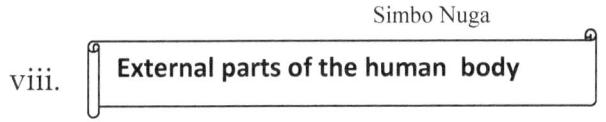

abdomen	Adam's apple	ankle	arm
breast	buttocks	calf	cheek
chest	chin	clitoris	earlobe
elbow	eye	ear	eyebrow
fingers	foot	forehead	groin
hair	hand	head	heel
hip	instep	jaw	knee
knuckle	leg	lip	mole
mouth	navel	neck	nose
penis	palm	little finger	ring finger
scrotum	shoulders	sole	spine
teeth	temple	nostrils	thigh
thorax	throat	thumb	toes
thigh	tongue	vulva	wrist

<u>Write more words below:</u>

ix. Financial terms

- audit
- bond
- capital
- debtor
- equity
- forecast
- gearing
- hedge
- interest
- journal
- kilo
- lease
- management
- neutral
- optimum
- profit
- quote
- revenue
- sales
- turnover
- unlisted
- variance
- wallet
- x-axis
- yield
- zero-based

x. **Names of fruits**

apricot
banana
coconut
durian
elderberry
fig
guava
honeysuckle
Indian prune
jackfruit
kiwi
lemon
mango
nectarine
orange
pineapple
quince
rhubarb
strawberry
tangerine
ugli fruit
vanilla fruit
watermelon
xylocarp
yuzu
ziziphus apple

Vocabulary: The personal Dictionary

xi. Types of games and sports

archery
basketball
cycling
diving
equestrianism
football
gymnastics
handball
ice hockey
judo
kayaking
lacrosse
motocross
netball
orienteering
polo
quoits
rugby
swimming
tennis
ultimate frisbee
volleyball
wrestling
xare
yachting
zorb football

xii.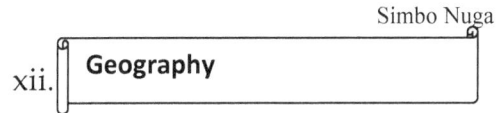

atlas	bedrock	canal	census
continent	conurbation	crater	delta
demography	dome	elevation	enclave
equator	estuary	fjord	glacier
gulf	hemisphere	horizon	island
jungle	lagoon	latitude	longitude
magma	map	mountain	ocean
palisades	pueblo	region	scale
smog	temperate	topography	tropics
valley	vent	volcano	water
weather	windward	zoning	

Write more words below:

xiii. **History**

chronology civil war colonial rule conservatism
emancipation of women Feudalism holocaust
mafia Mutiny of the bounty Nuremberg Trials
parliamentarian pilgrimage Pope puritan
revolution slavery timeline Titanic
U-boats United Nations Vietnam
Watergate World War II Ypres

Write more words below:

xiv. Things found in a house

attic	basement	bathroom	bathtub
bed	bedroom	blanket	book shelf
ceiling	chair	chest of drawers	
closet	coffee table	couch	cupboard
desk	door	dryer	dustbin
entrance	flower pot	floor	furniture
garden	garage	hallway	house
kitchen	living room	microwave	mirror
oven	pictures	pillow	radio
refrigerator	rocking chair	room	sink
shed	stove	table	tap
television	toilet	vacuum cleaner	wall
washer	window		

Write more words below:

Vocabulary: The personal Dictionary

XV. Legal terms

- affidavit
- bail
- criminal
- defence
- embezzlement
- Fraud
- guardian
- high court
- indict
- judicial
- kidnap
- libel
- magistrate
- notary
- order
- perjury
- quorum
- repossess
- sanction
- trial
- ultra vires
- verdict
- warrant
- x-patent
- youth
- zero tape

xvi. **Literary terms**

- analogy
- ballad
- couplet
- dactyl
- epitaph
- fable
- genre
- haiku
- idioms
- juggernaut
- kabuki
- limerick
- metaphor
- novel
- onomatopoeia
- personification
- quatrain
- rhetorical question
- simile
- tercet
- understatement
- vernacular
- wit
- xenia
- yard
- zappai

Mathematics

algorithm	arithmetic	average	Axim
bar chart	calculus	circumference	concave
concentric	cone	congruent	cosine
cuboid	cylinder	decimal	degree
denominator	diameter	diamond	dividend
equation	equilateral	extrapolate	factor
factorise	Fibonacci series	formula	fraction
geometry	gradient	group	hypotenuse
Index	inequality	intercept	inverse
Isometric	kite	linear	logarithm
Lune	matrix	mean	median
Mode	normal	number	quotient
radius	ratio	reciprocal	rectangle
rhombus	root	rotation	scalene
sphere	skew	square	tangent
tessellation	trapezium	trigonometry	unit
variance	vector	vertex	zero

Write more words below:

xviii. **Medical terms**

abdomen
bacteria
cadaver
denture
embolism
forceps
gangrene
hernia
influenza
jaundice
kwashiorkor
laryngitis
malignant
nebuliser
oedema
pancreas
quinine
rabies
saliva
tendon
ulcer
vaccine
wheeze
xenophobia
y-linked
zygote

xix. Parts of an animal

back	barrel	cannon	chin
coronet	crest	croup	dock
elbow	ergot	eyes	fetlock
flank	forearm	gaskin	groove
head	hock	hoof	knee
latch	loin	muzzle	point of hip
poll	shoulder	stifle	tail
teeth	throat	tongue	withers

Write more words below:

xx. **Parts of a bird**

back	beak	belly	breast
comb	coverts	crown	face
hackles	leg	nap	nostrils
spur	tail	thigh	throat
toes with claws		upper tail	wattles
wings			

Write more words below:

xxi. **Terms used for family and friends**

associate	auntie	aunt	boy
boyfriend	brother	children	cousin
boss	colleague	daddy	daughter
extended family		father	female
friend	girl	girlfriend	grandad
grandfather	grandma	grandmother	grandpa
heir	husband	male	master
maternal	matriarch	Miss	mistress
mother	Mr.	Mrs.	Ms.
mummy	nana	neighbour	nephew
niece	nuclear family	partner	paternal
patriarch	sister	wife	

Write more words below:

xxii. **Places**

avenue	_____	_____
bridle path	_____	_____
close	_____	_____
drive	_____	_____
enclave	_____	_____
field	_____	_____
grove	_____	_____
hotel	_____	_____
inn	_____	_____
junction	_____	_____
Knightsbridge	_____	_____
lane	_____	_____
mansion	_____	_____
nest	_____	_____
orphanage	_____	_____
place	_____	_____
roundabout	_____	_____
street	_____	_____
terrace	_____	_____
university	_____	_____
vale	_____	_____
windmill	_____	_____
zoo	_____	_____

Vocabulary: The personal Dictionary

xxiii. **Professions**

architect
baker
choreographer
dentist
engineer
farmer
geologist
historian
interpreter
judge
kitchen fitter
librarian
mathematician
nutritionist
optician
painter
quantity surveyor
radiographer
stockbroker
technologist
upholsterer
vet
writer
x-ray technician
yoga instructor
zoologist

xxiv. Religions of the world

Atheism _____ _____
Buddhism _____ _____
Christianity _____ _____
Druze _____ _____
Epicureanism _____ _____
Falun Gong _____ _____
Gnosticism _____ _____
Hinduism _____ _____
Islam _____ _____
Judaism _____ _____
Kabbalah _____ _____
Lutheranism _____ _____
Mormonism _____ _____
Norse Religion _____ _____
Olmec Religion _____ _____
Paganism _____ _____
Rastafarian _____ _____
Scientology _____ _____
Taoism _____ _____
Unitarianism _____ _____
Voodoo _____ _____
Wicca _____ _____
Yezidism _____ _____
Zoroastrianism _____ _____

Vocabulary: The personal Dictionary

XXV. School (People and things)

assembly
blackboard
caretaker
desk
eraser
flag
grass
headmaster
infants
juniors
kite
library
mirror
nurse
office
playground
queue
radio
secretary
teacher
uniform
video
warden
xylophone
yardstick
zip

xxvi. Science

analog	bacteria	botany	carbohydrates
Celsius	chemistry	circuit	cyberspace
decibel	dynamo	elasticity	electro-volt
ethernet	Fahrenheit	frequency	friction
gigabytes	gravity	hypothesis	indicator
infrared light	insulator	internet	joule
keratin	luminosity	magnetism	nanosecond
nerve	nocturnal	oncogene	ovulation
parasitism	particle	Physics	planet
psychology	satellite	solar system	thermal gradient
time	uterus	velocity	vitamins
weight	X-chromosome		x-ray
Y-chromosome	yellow fever	zoology	

Write more words below:

xxvii. **Sewing**

armscye	bias	dart	embroidery
face	gather	gusset	haberdasher
hem	interfacing	jersey	lining
millinery	muslin	needlework	overlay
pleat	quilt	ruching	seam
stitch	surplice	thimble	trim
yarn			

Write more words below:

xxviii **Names of vegetables**

- asparagus _____ _____
- broccoli _____ _____
- cauliflower _____ _____
- dill _____ _____
- eggplant _____ _____
- French bean _____ _____
- gherkin _____ _____
- horseradish _____ _____
- iceberg lettuce _____ _____
- jalapeno pepper _____ _____
- kale _____ _____
- leek _____ _____
- mushroom _____ _____
- nopal _____ _____
- okra _____ _____
- pumpkin _____ _____
- quinoa _____ _____
- radish _____ _____
- sprouts _____ _____
- turnip _____ _____
- upland cress _____ _____
- velvet bean _____ _____
- watercress _____ _____
- yam _____ _____
- zucchini _____ _____

PART 4

Confusable Words

"Example is the best precept."

Aesop (c.620-560 BC)

Introduction

Some words are used incorrectly and often confused with others either because they are similar in sound, spelling or are close in meaning (See Table 1 on page 146). These words include homographs, homonyms and homophones. The explanation with examples of each term is provided below.

i. *Homographs* are words that may have the same spelling, (but not necessarily pronounced the same) and have different meanings and origins. Table 2, on page 148 provides some examples.

ii. *Homonyms* are words that have the same spelling or pronunciation but different meanings. Some examples with explanations are:

park - the act of leaving a car on the road; a designated communal grassland used for recreational purposes.

ball – a round object; a formal dance

band – a rock band; a rubber band

clip – to clip a hedge; a paper clip

bat - a piece of sporting equipment used in table tennis; a winged animal associated with vampires

Refer to table 3 on page 149 for some examples.

iii. *Homophones* are two or more words that have the same pronunciation but different meanings, origins, or spelling.

Examples are:

knew, new   *sow, sew cite, site, sight*
whether, weather   *to, two, too*
there, their, they're

Refer to Table 4 on page 151 for a list of homophones.

Vocabulary: The personal Dictionary

In order, not to confuse these types of words, it is worth remembering that *homo* as a prefix means *the same*. The only difference then is the suffix:

graph - refers to drawing and writing
nym- refers to names
phone - refers to sound or pronunciation

Some words are often confused with others and used inappropriately. Listed below are some of these words. The explanation in the brackets states the use of each word, and the list includes words that are contractions.

a lot (a large amount); *allot* (distribute, assign)
all ready (completely prepared); *already* (previously)
all together (all in one place); *altogether* (thoroughly)
all ways (all methods); *always* (at all times)
breath (noun); *breathe* (verb)
bring (moving toward); *take* (to carry off)
can (has the ability); *may* (has permission)
cloths (fabrics); *clothes* (garments)
envelope (noun); *envelop* (verb)
every day (each day); *everyday* (ordinary)
fewer (something you can count); *less* (something you can't count)
good (adjective); *well* (adverb)
human (of people); *humane* (merciful)
its (possessive pronoun); *it's* (it is)
later (after more time); *latter* (in final position)
lay (to place); *lie* (to recline or tell an untruth)
less (use before a singular word, e.g. *less milk*); *fewer* (use before a plural word, e.g., *fewer people*)
may be (could be); *maybe* (perhaps)
passed (from the verb *to pass*, e.g., He passed the ball to her.);
past (often follows a verb, e.g., I went past the cinema.)
sit (to rest the body); *set* (to place something)
some time (an amount of time); *sometime* (at some unspecified time)

such as (something is included); *like* (implies a preference for a thing)
they're (they are); *their* (of them) *there* (at that place)
who's (who is); *whose* (of whom)
which (one of several things); *who* (what person) *who* (subjects) *whom* (objects)
you're (you are); *your* (of you)

You are now required to learn and practise confusable words. Write a short sentence in the space provided in the box next to each word. The word usage template in Appendix 7 and the confusable word template in Appendix 8 are handy tools.

Here is an example.

classic		classical
Musa the doctor, thinks it was a classic case of dehydration.	Siobhan and Seyi like classical music.	

Do ensure that you check the dictionary for the meaning of any word that you are unsure of because in the words of Steve Maraboli, *"A lack of clarity could put the brakes on any journey to success*

lay		lie	
which		who	
fewer		less	

Vocabulary: The personal Dictionary

abrogate	arrogate
accede	exceed
accessary	accessory
activate	actuate
adduce	deduce
adverse	averse
affect	effect
all ready	already

allusive	elusive
ambiguous	ambivalent
assume	presume
authoritarian	authoritative
beneficence	benevolence
biannual	biennial
breath	breathe
cloths	clothes

Vocabulary: The personal Dictionary

continuously	continually
converse	inverse
council	counsel
defective	deficient
definite	definitive
defuse	diffuse
delusion	illusion
dependant	dependent

discreet			discrete
good			well
flaunt			flout
fictional			fictitious
fewer			less
explicit			implicit
expedient			expeditious
exhausting			exhaustive

Vocabulary: The personal Dictionary

exclude	preclude
erupt	irrupt
equable	equitable
equitable	equable
disinterested	uninterested
stimulant	stimulus
substantial	substantive
tragedy	travesty
truthful	trustworthy

sensibility	sensitivity
reversal	revision
imaginary	imaginative
militate	mitigate
naught	nought
official	officious
ostensible	ostentatious
principle	principal

Vocabulary: The personal Dictionary

nationalise	naturalise
remission	remittance
prevaricate	procrastinate
practical	practicable
seat	sit
who's	whose
you're	your
aesthetic	ascetic

antiquated	antique
alternately	alternatively
alteration	altercation
amiable	amicable
affluent	effluent
allegory	allergy
among	between
angel	angle

Vocabulary: The personal Dictionary

arisen	arose
base	bass
axes	axis
astrology	astronomy
bellow	below
bridle	bridal
broach	brooch
breach	breech
bizarre	bazaar

centenarian	centenary
complement	compliment
comma	coma
crevasse	crevice
cygnet	signet
currant	current
deer	dear
descendant	descendent

Vocabulary: The personal Dictionary

desert	dessert
dew	due
course	coarse
coop	coup
curtsy	courtesy
creak	creek
dairy	diary
doe	dough
draft	drought

expensive	expansive
eyrie	eerie
faint	feint
foreword	forward

Vocabulary: The personal Dictionary

Table 1 Confusable words

abroad/abroad	accept/except	access/excess
acme/acne	adapter/adaptor	addition/edition
adverse/averse	advice/advise	aesthetic/ascetic
affect/effect	affluent/effluent	ail/ale
air/heir	all/awl	allay/alley
allegory/allergy	alley/allay	alliterate/illiterate
allude/elude	allusion/delusion/illusion	altar/alter
alteration/altercation	alternatively/alternately	amateur/amateurish
amend/emend	amiable/amicable	among/between
angel/angle	antiquated/antique	arc/ark
arisen/arose	artist/artiste	ascent/assent
aural/oral	awl/all	axes/axis
bade/bad	bail/bale	baited/bated
bare/bear	base/bass	bawl/ball
bazaar/bizarre	beach/beech	bean/been
beer/bier	beet/beat	befallen/befell
began/begun	belief/believe	bell/belle
bellow/below	berth/birth	between/among
bier/beer	bight/bite	boar/boor
boost/boast	borough/burgh	bridal/bridle
cache/cash	cavalier/cavalry	cellular/cellulose
censor/censure	centenarian/centenary	cereal/serial
chafe/chaff	chartered/charted	cheap/cheep
chilly/chilli	choir/quire	chord/cord
chute/shoot	cite/site	coarse/course
coma/comma	complement/compliment	concert/consort
crevasse/crevice	confident/confidant	consul/council/counsel
coop/coup	coronet/cornet	cornflour/cornflower
corps/corpse	councillor/counsellor	creak/creek
curb/kerb	cygnet/signet	dear/deer
delusion/allusion	desert/dessert	devolution/evolution
dew/due	diary/dairy	die/dye
died/dyed	dinghy/dingy	discus/discuss
doe/dough	dully/duly	dungeon/dudgeon
eclipse/ellipse	effluent/affluent	elicit/illicit
eligible/legible	emend/amend	emigrant/immigrant
emission/omission	emphasis/emphasize	ensure/insure
epigram/epitaph	evolution/devolution	ewe/yew
expand/expend	expatiate/expiate	expend/expand
fain/feign	faint/feint	fare/fair
faun/fawn	final/finale	fission/fissure
flare/flare	flew/flu	flocks/phlox
foment/ferment	foreword/forward	forswore/forsworn

forth/fourth	freeze/frieze	funeral/funereal
fur/fir	galleon/gallon	gate/gait
genie/genius	genteel/gentile	goal/gaol
gorilla/guerrilla	gourmand/gourmet	gradation/graduation
guerrilla/gorilla	hart/heart	heron/herring
hoarse/horse	hoop/whoop	horde/hoard
hue/hew	illicit/elicit	impetuous/impetus
inapt/inept	indigenous/indigent	ingenious/ingenuous
invertebrate/inveterate		judicial/judicious
knave/nave	knit/nit/neat	knotty/naughty
lay/lie	latterly/laterally	lemming/lemon
lessen/lesson	liable/libel	liar/lyre
lumber/lumbar	lute/loot	macaroni/macaroon
made/maid	magnate/magnet	main/mane
maniac/manic	marshal/martial	mask/masque
medal/meddle	meet/meat	meter/metre
mite/might	momentary/momentous	morality/mortality
moat/mote	mucous/mucus	muscle/mussel
mystic/mystique	naught/nought	naughty/knotty
naval/navel	need/knead	negligent/negligible
nightly/knightly	nougat/nugget	oar/ore official/officious
omission/emission	pail/pale	palate/palette
pare/pear/pair	peasant/pheasant	pedal/peddle
peel/peal	pendent/pendant	prerequisite/perquisite
personal/personnel	pizza/piazza	piece/peace
pique/peak	pistil/pistol	plaintiff/plaintive
plate/plait	pool/pull	pore/pour
pray/prey	precede/proceed	prise/price
private/privet	profit/prophet	proof/prove
property/propriety	prostate/prostrate	quash/squash
quay/key	queue/cue	quire/choir
racket/racquet	raider/radar	rain/reign/rein
rote/wrote	rough/ruff	rout/route
rung/wrung	rye/wry	sceptic/septic
sealing/ceiling	sear/seer	sensual/sensuous
septic/sceptic	sinuous/sinus	slay/sleigh
soar/sore	staid/stayed	stanch/staunch
tare/tear	team/teem	temporal/temporary
their/there	thorough/through	throne/thrown
thyme/time	tier/tear	treaties/treatise
troop/troupe	turban/turbine	tycoon/typhoon
vacation/vocation	vertex/vortex	wafer/waver
yolk/yoke		

Table 2 Homographs

agape (wide open; Greek word meaning love)
ball (a round object; a formal dance)
band (a rock band; a rubber band)
bass (deep voice; a kind of fish)
bat (a piece of sporting equipment used in table tennis; a winged animal associated with vampires
bow (to bend at the waist; a pair of tied loops)
clip (to clip a hedge; a paper clip)
content (happy and satisfied; all that is contained inside a thing)
down (in a lower position; furry feathers)
evening (late afternoon; making more equal)
fine (delicate or subtle; an amount paid to settle a matter)
lead (a type of metal; to head a group of followers)
minute (sixty seconds; very small)
object (something concrete; to be opposed to a decision   or act)
park (the act of leaving a car on the road; a designated communal grassland used for recreational purposes)
produce (to create or make; fresh fruits and vegetables)

Table 3 Homonyms

accept (receive); *except* (leave out)
affect (influence, verb); *effect* (result, noun)
allowed (permitted); *aloud* (clearly heard)
ate (past tense of eat); *eight* (the number)
break (smash, split); *brake* (stopping device)
by (preposition); *buy* (purchase)
capital (city, wealth); *capitol* (building)
cite (mention); *sight* (vision)
coarse (rough); *course* (way or path)
complement (make complete); *compliment* (praise)
conscience (moral judgment); *conscious* (aware)
council (committee); *counsel* (advice, adviser)
desert (dry land); *dessert* (sweet food)
do (to act); *dew* (moisture); *due* (deadline)
dual (having two parts); *duel* (fight)
dye (colour); *die* (perish)
faze (disturb, bother); *phase* (stage)
for (preposition); *four* (number)
forth (forward); *fourth* (comes after third)
hear (perceive); *here* (in this place)
heard (perceived); *herd* (group)
heroin (drug); *heroine* (main female character)
hole (opening); *whole* (entire)
knot (twist); *not* (negative)
know (be aware); *no* (opposite of yes)
knows (be aware); *nose* (part of face)
lead (metal); *led* (guided)
loose (free, united); *lose* (misplace, fail to win)
meat (food); *meet* (encounter)
metal (element); *medal* (award)
miner (excavator); *minor* (young person)
one (less than two); *won* (to acquire)
passed (went by); *past* (earlier time)
peace (absence of war); *piece* (part, portion)
plain (simple); *plane* (flat surface)
poor (not rich); *pour* (liquids); *pore* (opening in skin)
principle (rule); *principal* (chief person, sum)
quiet (silent); *quite* (really, positively)
rain (precipitation); *reign* (rule, authority)
read (process words); *red* (colour)
right (proper); *rite* (ritual); *write* (put pen to paper)

Vocabulary: The personal Dictionary

road (path); *rowed* (a boat); *rode* (past tense of ride)
scene (stage, setting); *seen* (perceived)
sense (perception); *since* (from that time)
stationary (not moving); *stationery* (writing paper)
straight (not curved); *strait* (narrow place)
threw (past tense of throw); *through* (by way of)
to (in the direction of); *two* (number); *too* (also)
waist (centre of body); *waste* (squander)
weak (feeble); *week* (seven days)
wear (carry on the body); *where* (in what place)
weather (atmospheric conditions); *whether* (if, in case)
which (what one); *witch* (sorceress)

Table 4 Homophones

A

air, heir   aisle, I'll, isle   allowed, aloud   alms, arms
altar, alter   arc, ark   aren't, aunt   ate, eight
auger, augur   aural, oral   away, aweigh   awe, oar, or, ore
axel, axle   eye, I

B

bail, bale   bait, bate   baize, bays
bald, balled, bawled   ball, bawl   band, banned
bard, barred   bare, bear   bark, barque   baron, barren
base, bass   bay, bey   bazaar, bizarre   be, bee
beach, beech   bean, been   beat, beet   beau, bow
beer, bier   bell, belle   berry, bury   berth, birth
bight, bite, byte   billed, build   bitten, bittern   blew, blue
bloc, block   boar, bore   board, bored   boarder, border
bold, bowled   boos, booze   born, borne   bough, bow
boy, buoy   brae, bray   braid, brayed
braise, brays, braze   brake, break   bread, bred
brews, bruise   bridal, bridle   broach, brooch   but, butt
buy, by, bye   buyer, byre

C

cache, cash   cachou, cashew   caddie, caddy   call, caul
came, kame   canvas, canvass   cast, caste   caster, castor
caught, court   cede, seed   ceiling, sealing   cell, sell
censer, censor, sensor   cent, scent, sent   cereal, serial
cheap, cheep   check, cheque   choir, quire   chord, cord
cite, sight, site   clack, claque   clew, clue
close, cloze   coal, kohl   coarse, course   colonel, kernel
complement, compliment   coo, coup   cops, copse
council, counsel   cousin, cozen   creak, creek
crews, cruise   cue, queue   curb, kerb
currant, current   cymbal, symbol

D

dam, damn   days, daze   dear, deer   descent, dissent
desert, dessert   deviser, divisor   dew, due   die, dye
discreet, discrete   doe, dough   done, dun   douse, dowse
draft, draught   dual, duel

E

earn, urn   ewe, yew, you

Vocabulary: The personal Dictionary

F

faint, feint	fair, fare	farther, father	fate, fête
faun, fawn	faze, phase	feat, feet	ferrule, ferule
few, phew	file, phial	find, fined	fir, fur
flair, flare	flaw, floor	flea, flee	flew, flu, flue
flex, flecks	floe, flow	flour, flower	foaled, fold
for, fore, four	fort, fought	forth, fourth	foul, fowl
furs, furze	franc, frank	freeze, frieze	friar, fryer

G

gait, gate	genes, jeans	gild, guild	gilt, guilt
giro, gyro	gnaw, nor	gneiss, nice	gorilla, guerrilla
grate, great	greys, graze	grisly, grizzly	groan, grown
guessed, guest			

H

hail, hale	hair, hare	hall, haul	hangar, hanger
hart, heart	haw, hoar, whore	hay, hey	heal, heel, he'll
hear, here	heard, herd	he'd, heed	heroin, heroine
hew, hue	hi, high	higher, hire	him, hymn
ho, hoe	hoard, horde	hoarse, horse	holey, holy, wholly
hour, our			

I

idle, idol	in, inn	it's, its	

J

jewel, joule

K

key, quay	knave, nave	knead, need	knew, new
knight, night	knit, nit	knob, nob	knot, not
know, no	knows, nose		

L

laager, lager	lac, lack	lade, laid	lain, lane
lam, lamb	laps, lapse	larva, lava	law, lore
lay, ley	lea, lee	leach, leech	lead, led
leak, leek	lean, lien	lessen, lesson	levee, levy
liar, lyre	licence, license	licker, liquor	lie, lye
links, lynx	lo, low	load, lode	loan, lone
locks, lox	loop, loupe	loot, lute	

M

made, maid   mail, male   main, mane   maize, maze
mall, maul   manna, manner   mantel, mantle   mare, mayor
mark, marque   marshal, martial   marten, martin   mask, masque
maw, more   meat, meet, mete   medal, meddle   metal, mettle
meter, metre   might, mite   mind, mined   miner, minor
missed, mist   moat, mote   mode, mowed   moor, more
moose, mousse   morning, mourning   muscle, mussel

N

naval, navel   nay, neigh   none, nun

O

ode, owed   oh, owe   one, won

P

packed, pact   pail, pale   pain, pane   pair, pare, pear
palate, pallet   pascal, paschal   pause, paws,   pores, pours
peace, piece   peak, peek, pique   peal, peel   pearl, purl
pedal, peddle   peer, pier   pi, pie   place, plaice
plain, plane   pleas, please   plum, plumb   poof, pouf
practice, practise   praise, prays, preys   principal, principle   profit, prophet

Q

quarts, quartz   quean, queen

R

rain, reign, rein   raise, rays, raze   rap, wrap   raw, roar
read, reed   read, red   real, reel   reek, wreak
rest, wrest   retch, wretch   review, revue   rheum, room
right, rite, wright, write   ring, wring   road, rode
roe, row   role, roll   roux, rue   rood, rude
root, route   rose, rows   rota, rotor   rote, wrote
rough, ruff   rouse, rows   rung, wrung   rye, wry

S

saver, savour   sale, sail   sane, seine   sauce, source
swat, swot   saw, soar, sore   scene, seen   scull, skull
sea, see   seam, seem   sear, seer, sere   seas, sees, seize
sew, so, sow   shake, sheikh   shear, sheer   shoe, shoo
side, sighed   sign, sine   sink, synch   slay, sleigh

Vocabulary: The personal Dictionary

sloe, slow   sole, soul   some, sum   son, sun
sort, sought   spa, spar   spade, spayed   staid, stayed
stair, stare   stake, steak   stationary, stationery
steal, steel   stile, style   storey, story   straight, strait
sweet, suite

T

tacks, tax   tale, tail   talk, torque   tare, tear
taught, taut, tort   tea, tee   team, teem   tear, tier
tern, turn   there, their, they're   threw, through   throes, throws
throne, thrown   thyme, time   tide, tied
tire, tyre   to, too, two   toad, toed, towed   told, tolled
tough, tuff   troop, troupe   tuba, tuber

V

vain, vane, vein   vale, veil,   vial, vile

W

wail, wale, whale   wain, wane   waist, waste   wait, weight
waive, wave   war, wore   ware, wear, where   warn, worn
wart, wort   watt, what   wax, whacks   way, weigh, whey
we, wee   weak, week   weal, we'll, wheel   wean, ween
weather, whether   weaver, waiver   weir, we're   were, whirr
wet, whet   wield, wheeled   which, witch   while, wile
whine, wine   whirl, who   whirled, world   whit, wit
white, Wight   who's, whose   woe, whoa   wood, would

Y

yaw, yore, your, you're   yoke, yolk   you'll, yule

PART 5
Reference Materials

*Patience, persistence, and perseverance.
A little more each day, a little better each day.
- Jonathan Lockwood Huie*

Vocabulary: The personal Dictionary

Introduction

This part of the book consists of the following useful reference materials: names of the days of the week, names and the number of days in each month of the year, expressions of time, names of the seasons, names of things we cannot count, the correct spelling of numbers, roman numerals and a detailed list of the names of animals. The animal names include the name given to the parent, male, female and their young. This list is followed by the names of countries, their respective citizens, capital cities, languages and currencies, roman numerals, prefixes and suffixes.

a. Days of the week

Monday Tuesday Wednesday Thursday Friday
Saturday Sunday

b. Names of months and number of days

Month	Number of Days
January	31
February	28 or 29
March	31
April	30
May	31
June	30
July	31
August	31
September	30
October	31
November	30
December	31

c. Expressions of time

Second	Base unit
Minute	60 seconds
Hour	60 minutes
Day	24 hours
Week	7 days
Fortnight	14 day
Lunar Months	27.2 – 29.5 days
February	28 – 29 days
Common Month	30 – 31 days
Quarter/Seasons	3 months
Year	12 months
Common Year	365 days
Leap Year	366 days
Biennium	2 years
Triennium	3 years
Olympiad	4-year cycle
Lustrum	5 years
Decade	10 years
Jubilee	50 years
Life Span	About 85 years
Century	100 years
Millennium	1000 Years

d. Names of seasons

Autumn/Fall	Dry season	Harmattan	
Rainy season	Spring	Summer	Winter

e. Colours

black	blue	brown	gold	green
grey	orange	pink	purple	red
silver	yellow	white	red-orange	yellow-orange
yellow-green		blue-green	blue-violet	red-violet

f. Things we cannot count

Food and Drink	Thoughts/Emotions	Everyday/ Miscellaneous Things	
alcohol	anger	air	mail
beef	aggression	accommodation	mud
bread	assistance	applause	nature
blood	bemusement	art	paper
butter	bravery	attention	petrol
cheese	curiosity	baggage	poetry
chocolate	courage	business	rain
cream	faith	chess	sunshine
fruit	freedom	currency	time
flour	fun	dust	traffic
honey	greed	dirt	travel
juice	grief	education	yoga
milk	guilt	entertainment	
oil	happiness	equipment	
pasta	humour	grass	
pork	insincerity	heat	
rice	knowledge	homework	
salt	love	ink	
sugar	satisfaction	judo	
syrup		land	
tea		literature	
water		lotion	
wine			
vinegar			

g. Animals: Parent, Young, Male and Female

Animal	Female	Male	Young

A
Alligator	cow	bull	hatchling
Ant	queen, princess	prince, drone	antling
Antelope	cow	bull	calf, fawn, kid
Ass	jenny	jack, jackass	foal

B
Badger	sow	boar	cub
Bear	sow, she-bear	boar, he-bear	cub
Beaver			kit, kitten, pup
Bee	queen,	drone	larva
Bird	hen	cock	hatchling, chick
Bison	cow	bull	calf
Boar (wild)	sow	boar	boarlet, shoat, farrow
Bobcat			kitten or cub
Buffalo	cow	bull	calf or spike-bull

C
Camel	cow	bull	calf or colt
Canary	hen	cock	chick
Caribou	cow, doe	bull, stag, hart	calf or fawn
Cat	dam, queen	tomcat, gib	kitten
Cattle	cow	bull	calf (m. bull calf or f. heifer)
Chicken	hen,	cock, rooster	chick, poult, cockerel
Cicada			nymph
Cod			codling, scrod, or sprag
Cougar	she-cougar	tom	kitten or cub
Coyote	bitch	dog	whelp, pup
Crocodile		bull	hatchling

D
Deer	hind, doe	buck, stag	fawn
Dog	bitch	dog	puppy
Dolphin	cow	bull	calf, pup
Dove	hen	cock	pigeon or squab
Duck	duck	drake	duckling or flapper

Vocabulary: The personal Dictionary

Animal	Female	Male	Young
E			
Eagle			eaglet, fledgling
Echidna			puggle
Eel			fry or elver
Elephant	cow	bull	calf
Elk	cow	bull	calf
F			
Ferret	hob	jill	kit
Fish			fry, minnow or spawn
Fly			grub or maggot
Fox	vixen, she-fox	fox, reynard	kit, cub, pup
Frog			tadpole, froglet
G			
Giraffe	cow	bull	calf
Goat	nanny, she-goat	billy, he-goat	kid
Goose	goose, dame	gander, stag	gosling
Gorilla	black back	silverback	infant
Grouse			chick, squealer
Guinea pig	sow	boar	pup
H			
Hare	jill	jack	leveret
Hawk	hen	tiercel	eyas
Hedgehog	sow	boar	pup, piglet
Hippopotamus	cow	bull	calf
Horse	mare	stallion, stag	foal, colt (m), filly (f)
I			
Impala	ewe	ram	
K			
Kangaroo	doe	buck	joey
L			
Leopard	leopardess	leopard	cub
Lion	lioness, she-lion	lion	cub or
Lobster	hen	cock	
Louse			nit

Simbo Nuga

Animal	Female	Male	Young
M			
Manatee	cow	bull	calf
Mink	sow	boar	kit or cub
Monkey			suckling, yearling or infant
Moose	cow	bull	calf
Mosquito			larva, nymph
Mouse	doe	buck	pup, kitten
Mule	she-ass, more	stallion	foal
Muskrat			kit
O			
Opossum	jill	jack	joey
Ostrich	hen	cock	chick
Otter	bitch	dog	pup, kitten, whelp or cub
Owl	jenny		owlet
Ox	cow, beef	ox, beef	stot, calf
Oyster			spat or brood
P			
Partridge	hen	cock	cheeper
Peacock	hen, pea-hen	cock, peacock	chick, pea-chick
Pelican			chick, nestling
Penguin	hen	cock	fledgling, chick
Pheasant	hen	cock	chick, poult
Pig	sow	boar	shoat, farrow, piglet
Pigeon	hen	cock	squab, nestling, squealer
Platypus			puggle
Possum	jill	jack	joey
Q			
Quail	hen	cock	chick, squealer
R			
Rabbit	doe	buck	kitten, bunny
Raccoon	sow	boar	kit, cub
Rat	doe	buck	kitten, pup
Reindeer	doe	buck	fawn
Rhinoceros	cow	bull	calf
Robin	hen	cock	

Vocabulary: The personal Dictionary

Animal	Female	Male	Young
S			
Salmon	hen	jack	salmon parr, smolts, fry
Sea Lion	cow	bull	pup
Seal	cow	bull	whelp, pup, cub, bachelor
Shark	cow	bull	pup
Sheep	ewe, dam	ram, mutton	lamb or yearling
Skunk		boar	kitten
Squirrel	doe	buck	kitten
Swan	pen	cob	cygnet, flapper
Swine	sow	boar	shoat, trotter, pig or piglet
T			
Termite	queen	king	nymph
Tiger	tigress	tiger	whelp, cub
Toad			tadpole
Trout	hen	jack	fry
Turkey	hen	gobbler, tom	chick
W			
Walrus	cow	bull	cub
Weasel	bitch, doe, jill	dog, buck, hob	kit
Whale	cow	bull	calf
Wolf	bitch	dog	cub, pup
Woodchuck	she-chuck	he-chuck	kit, cub
Z			
Zebra	mare	stallion	foal, colt (m), fill

h. Countries, Citizens Capitals, Currencies And Languages

Country	Citizens	Capital(s)	Currency	Primary Language(s)
Afghanistan	Afghan	Kabul	Afghani	Dari Persian; Pashto
Albania	Albanian	Tirana	Lek	Albanian
Algeria	Algerian	Algiers	Algerian Dinar	Arabic; Tamazight; French
Andorra	Andorran	Andorra La Vella	Euro	Catalan
Angola	Angolan	Luanda	Kwanza	Portuguese
Antigua & Barbuda	Antiguan	Saint John's	East Caribbean Dollar	English
Argentina	Argentinian	Buenos Aires	Argentine Peso	Spanish
Armenia	Armenian	Yerevan	Dram	Armenian
Australia	Australian	Canberra	Australian Dollar	English
Austria	Austrian	Vienna	Euro	German
Azerbaijan	Azerbaijan	Baku	Manat	Azerbaijani
The Bahamas	Bahamian	Nassau	Bahamian Dollar	English
Bahrain	Bahraini	Manama	Bahraini Dinar	Arabic
Bangladesh	Bangladeshi	Dhaka	Taka	Bangla
Barbados	Barbadian	Bridgetown	Barbadian Dollar	English
Belarus	Belarussian	Minsk	Belarusian Ruble	Belarusian; Russian
Belgium	Belgian	Brussels	Euro	Dutch; French; German
Belize	Belizean	Belmopan	Belize Dollar	English
Benin	Beninese	Porto-Novo	West African CFA Franc	French
Bhutan	Bhutanese	Thimphu	Ngultrum	Dzongkha
Bolivia	Bolivian	La Paz; Sucre	Boliviano	Spanish; Quechua; Aymara
Bosnia And Herzegovina	Bosnian	Sarajevo	Convertible Mark	Bosnian; Croatian; Serbian
Botswana	Botswanan	Gaborone	Pula	English; Tswana
Brazil	Brazilian	Brasilia	Real	Portuguese
Brunei	Bruneian	Bandar Seri Begawan	Brunei Dollar	Malay
Bulgaria	Bulgarian	Sofia	Lev	Bulgarian
Burkina Faso	Burkinabe	Ouagadougou	West African CFA Franc	French
Burundi	Burundian	Bujumbura	Burundi Franc	Kirundi; French
Cambodia	Cambodian	Phnom Penh	Riel	Khmer
Cameroon	Cameroonian	Yaoundé	Central African CFA Franc	French; English
Canada	Canadian	Ottawa	Canadian Dollar	English; French
Cape Verde	Cape Verdean	Praia	Cape Verdean Escudo	Portuguese
Central African Republic	Central African	Bangui	Central African CFA Franc	Sango; French

Vocabulary: The personal Dictionary

Country	Citizens	Capital(s)	Currency	Primary Language(s)
Chad	Chadian	N'Djamena	Central African CFA Franc	French; Arabic
Chile	Chilean	Santiago	Chilean Peso	Spanish
China	Chinese	Beijing	Chinese Yuan	Mandarin
Colombia	Colombian	Bogota	Colombian Peso	Spanish
Comoros	Comorian	Moron	Comorian Franc	Comorian; Arabic; French
Democratic Republic of Congo	Congolese	Kinshasa	Congolese Franc	French
Republic Of The Congo	Congolese	Brazzaville	Central African CFA Franc	French
Costa Rica	Costa Rican	San Jose	Colon	Spanish
Cote D' Ivoire (Ivory Coast)	Ivorian	Yamoussoukro; Abidjan	West African CFA Franc	French
Croatia	Croatian	Zagreb	Croatian	Kuna
Cuba	Cuban	Havana	Cuban Peso	Spanish
Cyprus	Cypriot	Nicosia	Euro	Greek; Turkish
Czech Republic	Czech	Prague	Czech Koruna	Czech; Slovak
Denmark	Danish	Copenhagen	Danish Krone	Danish
Djibouti	Djiboutian	Djibouti	Djiboutian Franc	Arabic; French
Dominica	Dominican	Roseau	East Caribbean Dollar	English; French; Antillean Creole
Dominican Republic	Dominican	Santo Domingo	Dominican Peso	Spanish
East Timor (Timor-Leste)	East Timorese	Dili	United States Dollar	Tetum; Portuguese; Indonesian
Ecuador	Ecuadorean	Quito	United States Dollar	Spanish
Egypt	Egyptian	Cairo	Egyptian Pound	Arabic
El Salvador	El Salvadorian	San Salvador	United States Dollar	Spanish
Equatorial Guinea	Equatoguinean	Malabo	Central African CFA Franc	Spanish; French; Portuguese
Eritrea	Eritrean	Asmara	Nakfa	Arabic; Tigrinya; English
Estonia	Estonian	Tallinn	Estonian Kroon; Euro	Estonian
Ethiopia	Ethiopian	Addis Ababa	Birr	Amharic
Fiji	Fijian	Suva	Fijian Dollar	English; Bau Fijian; Hindi
Finland	Finnish	Helsinki	Euro	Finnish; Swedish
France	French	Paris	Euro; CFP Franc	French
Gabon	Gabonese	Libreville	Central African CFA Franc	French
The Gambia	Gambian	Banjul	Dalasi	English
Georgia	Georgian	Tbilisi	Lari	Georgian
Germany	German	Berlin	Euro	German
Ghana	Ghanaian	Accra	Ghanaian Cedi	English
Greece	Greek	Athens	Euro	Greek
Grenada	Grenadian	St. George's	East Caribbean Dollar	English; Patois

Country	Citizens	Capital(s)	Currency	Primary Language(s)
Guatemala	Guatemalan	Guatemala City	Quetzal	Spanish
Guinea	Guinean	Conakry	Guinean Franc	French
Guinea-Bissau	Bissau Guinean	Bissau	West African CFA Franc	Portuguese
Guyana	Guyanese	Georgetown	Guyanese Dollar	English
Haiti	Haitian	Port-Au-Prince	Gourde	Haitian Creole; French
Honduras	Honduran	Tegucigalpa	Lempira	Spanish
Hungary	Hungarian	Budapest	Forint	Hungarian
Iceland	Icelandic	Reykjavik	Icelandic Krona	Icelandic
India	Indian	New Delhi	Indian Rupee	Hindi; English
Indonesia	Indonesian	Jakarta	Rupiah	Indonesian
Iran	Iranian	Tehran	Rial	Persian
Iraq	Iraqi	Baghdad	Iraqi Dinar	Arabic; Kurdish
Republic Of Ireland	Irish	Dublin	Euro	English; Irish
Israel	Israeli	Jerusalem	Shekel	Hebrew; Arabic
Italy	Italian	Rome	Euro	Italian
Jamaica	Jamaican	Kingston	Jamaican Dollar	English
Japan	Japanese	Tokyo	Yen	Japanese
Jordan	Jordanian	Amman	Jordanian Dinar	Arabic
Kazakhstan	Kazakhstani	Astana	Tenge	Kazakh; Russian
Kenya	Kenyan	Nairobi	Kenyan Shilling	Swahili; English
Kiribati	Kiribatian	Tarawa Atoll	Kiribati Dollar	English; Gilbertese
North Korea	Korean	Pyongyang	North Korean Won	Korean
South Korea	Korean	Seoul	South Korean Won	Korean
Kosovo	Kosovan	Pristina	Euro	Albanian; Serbian
Kuwait	Kuwaiti	Kuwait City	Kuwaiti Dollar	Arabic; English
Kyrgyzstan	Kyrgyz	Bishkek	Som	Kyrgyz; Russian
Laos	Laotian	Vientiane	Kip	Lao (Laotian)
Latvia	Latvian	Riga	Lats	Latvian
Lebanon	Lebanese	Beirut	Lebanese Pound	Arabic; French
Lesotho	Basotho/ Mosotho	Maseru	Loti	Sesotho; English
Liberia	Liberian	Monrovia	Liberian Dollar	English
Libya	Libyan	Tripoli	Libyan Dinar	Arabic
Liechtenstein	Liechtenstein-er	Vaduz	Swiss Franc	German
Lithuania	Lithuanian	Vilnius	Euro	Lithuanian
Luxembourg	Luxembourger	Luxembourg	Euro	German; French; Luxembourgish
Macedonia	Macedonian	Skopje	Macedonian Dinar	Macedonian
Madagascar	Malagasy	Antananarivo	Malagasy Ariary	Malagasy; French; English
Malawi	Malawian	Lilongwe	Malawi Kwacha	English
Malaysia	Malaysian	Kuala Lumpur	Ringgit	Malay
Maldives	Maldivian	Male	Maldivian Rufiyaa	Dhivehi
Mali	Malian	Bamako	West African CFA Franc	French
Malta	Maltese	Valletta	Euro	Maltese; English
Marshall Islands	Marshall Islander	Majuro	United States Dollar	Marshallese; English
Mauritania	Mauritanian	Nouakchott	Ouguiya	Arabic

Vocabulary: The personal Dictionary

Country	Citizens	Capital(s)	Currency	Primary Language(s)
Mauritius	Mauritian	Port Louis	Mauritian Rupee	English
Mexico	Mexican	Mexico City	Mexican Peso	Spanish
Federal States Of Micronesia	Micronesian	Palikir	United States Dollar	English
Moldova	Moldovan	Chisinau	Moldovan Leu	Moldovan (Romanian)
Monaco	Monacan	Monaco	Euro	French; Italian; English
Mongolia	Mongolian	Ulaanbaatar	Togrog	Mongolian
Montenegro	Montenegrin	Podgorica	Euro	Montenegrin
Morocco	Moroccan	Rabat	Moroccan Dirham	Arabic
Mozambique	Mozambican	Maputo	Mozambican Metical	Portuguese
Myanmar (Burma)	Burmese	Naypyidaw	Kyat	Burmese
Namibia	Namibian	Windhoek	Namibian Dollar	English; Afrikaans; German
Nauru	Nauruan	Yaren	Australian Dollar	English; Nauran
Nepal	Nepali	Kathmandu	Nepalese Rupee	Nepali
Netherlands	Dutch	Amsterdam; The Hague	Euro	Dutch
New Zealand	New Zealander	Wellington	New Zealand Dollar	English
Nicaragua	Nicaraguan	Managua	Cordoba	Spanish
Niger	Nigerien	Niamey	West African CFA Franc	French
Nigeria	Nigerian	Abuja	Naira	English
Norway	Norwegian	Oslo	Norwegian Krone	Norwegian
Oman	Omani	Muscat	Omani Rial	Arabic
Pakistan	Pakistani	Islamabad	Pakistani Rupee	Urdu; English
Palau	Palauan	Melekeok	United States Dollar	English; Palauan
Panama	Panamanian	Panama City	Balboa	Spanish
Papa New Guinea	Papua New Guinean	Port Moresby Papa	Papa New Guinean Kina	English; TokPisin; Hiri Motu
Paraguay	Paraguayan	Asuncion	Guarani	Spanish; Guarani
Peru	Peruvian	Lima	Nuevo Sol	Spanish
Philippines	Filipino	Manila	Philippine Peso	Filipino; English
Poland	Polish	Warsaw	Zloty	Polish
Portugal	Portuguese	Lisbon	Euro	Portuguese
Qatar	Qatari	Doha	Qatari Riyal	Arabic
Romania	Romanian	Bucharest	Romanian Rupee	Romanian
Russia	Russian	Moscow	Ruble	Russian
Rwanda	Rwandan	Kigali	Rwandan Franc	Kinyarwanda; French; English
Saint Kitts And Nevis	Kittitian/Nevisian	Basseterre	East Caribbean Dollar	English
Saint Lucia	Saint Lucian	Castries	East Caribbean Dollar	English; French
Saint Vincent And The Grenadines	Vincentian/ Vincy	Kingstown East	Caribbean Dollar	English
Samoa	Samoan	Apia	Tala	Samoan; English
San Marino	Sammarinese	San Marino	Euro	Italian

Country	Citizens	Capital(s)	Currency	Primary Language(s)
Sao Tome And Principe	Sao Tomean	Sao Tome	Dobra	Portuguese
Saudi Arabia	Saudi	Riyadh	Saudi Riyal	Arabic
Senegal	Senegalese	Dakar	West African CFA Franc	French
Serbia	Serbian	Belgrade	Serbian Dinar	Serbian
Seychelles	Seychellois/e	Victoria	Seychellois Rupee	Seychellois Creole; French; English
Sierra Leone	Sierra Leonean	Freetown	Leone	Krio; English
Singapore	Singaporean	Singapore	Singapore Dollar	English; Malay; Mandarin Chinese
Slovakia	Slovak	Bratislava	Euro	Slovak
Slovenia	Slovene	Ljubljana	Euro	Slovene
Solomon Islands	Solomon Islander	Honiara	Solomon Islands Dollar	Solomon's Pijin
Somalia	Somalian	Mogadishu	Somali Shilling	Somali; Arabic
South Africa	South African	Pretoria; Cape Town; Bloemfontein	Rand	Zulu; Xhosa; Afrikaans
Spain	Spanish	Madrid	Euro	Spanish
Sri Lanka	Sri Lankan	Colombo	Sri Lankan Rupee	Sinhala; Tamil
Sudan	Sudanese	Khartoum	Sudanese Pound	Arabic; English
Suriname	Surinamese	Paramaribo	Surinamese Dollar	Dutch
Swaziland	Swazi	Mbabane	Lilangeni	English; SiSwati
Sweden	Swedish	Stockholm	Swedish Krona	Swedish
Switzerland	Swiss	Berne	Swiss Franc	German; French; Italian
Syria	Syrian	Damascus	Syrian Pound	Arabic
Taiwan	Taiwanese	Taipei	New Taiwan Dollar	Mandarin
Tajikistan	Tajik	Dushanbe	Somoni	Tajik; Russian
Tanzania	Tanzanian	Dar Es Salaam; Dodoma	Tanzanian Schilling	Swahili
Thailand	Thai	Bangkok	Thai Baht	Thai
Togo	Togolese	Lome	West African CFA Franc	French
Tonga	Tongan	Nuku'alofa	Pa'anga	Tongan; English
Trinidad And Tobago	Trinidadian/ Tobagonian	Port-Of-Spain	Trinidad And Tobago Dollar	English
Tunisia	Tunisian	Tunis	Tunisian Dinar	Tunisian; French
Turkey	Turkish	Ankara	Turkish Lira	Turkish
Turkmenistan	Turkmen	Ashgabat	Turkmen New Manat	Turkmen; Russian
Tuvalu	Tuvaluan	Vaitkus	Tuvaluan Dollar	Tuvaluan; English
Uganda	Ugandan	Kampala	Ugandan Shilling	Swahili; English
Ukraine	Ukrainian	Kiev	Hryvnia	Ukrainian; Russian
United Arab Emirates	Arab	Abu Dhabi	Dirham	Arabic
United Kingdom	British	London	Pound Sterling	English
United States Of America	American	Washington D.C.	United States Dollar	English; Spanish
Uruguay	Uruguayan	Montevideo	Uruguayan Peso	Spanish
Uzbekistan	Uzbekistani	Tashkent	Uzbekistan Som	Uzbek; Russian

Vocabulary: The personal Dictionary

Country	Citizens	Capital(s)	Currency	Primary Language(s)
Vanuatu	Ni Vanuatu	Port-Vila	Vanuatu Vatu	Bislama; English; French
Vatican City	Italian	Vatican City	Euro	Latin; Italian
Venezuela	Venezuelan	Caracas	Bolivar Fuertes	Spanish
Vietnam	Vietnamese	Hanoi	Dong	Vietnamese
Yemen	Yemeni	Sanaa	Yemeni Rial	Arabic
Zambia	Zambian	Lusaka	Zambian Kwacha	English
Zimbabwe	Zimbabwean	Harare	United States Dollar	English

i. Spelling Numbers

Cardinal number	**Ordinal number**
1 one	first
2 two	second
3 three	third
4 four	fourth
5 five	fifth
6 six	sixth
7 seven	seventh
8 eight	eighth
9 nine	ninth
10 ten	tenth
11 eleven	eleventh
12 twelve	twelfth
13 thirteen	thirteenth
14 fourteen	fourteenth
15 fifteen	fifteenth
16 sixteen	sixteenth
17 seventeen	seventeenth
18 eighteen	eighteenth
19 nineteen	nineteenth
20 twenty	twentieth
30 thirty	thirtieth
40 forty	fortieth
50 fifty	fiftieth
60 sixty	sixtieth
70 seventy	seventieth
80 eighty	eightieth
90 ninety	ninetieth
100 one hundred	one hundredth
1000 one thousand	one thousandth

j. Roman Numerals

Number	Roman Numeral
1	I
2	II
3	III
4	IV
5	V
6	VI
7	VII
8	VIII
9	IX
10	X
11	XI
12	XII
13	XIII
14	XIV
15	XV
16	XVI
17	XVII
18	XVIII
19	XIX
20	XX
30	XXX
40	XL
50	L
60	LX
70	LXX
80	LXXX
90	XC
100	C
200	CC
300	CCC
400	CD
500	D
600	DC
700	DCC
800	DCCC
900	CM
1000	M
5000	$\overline{V}$
10,000	$\overline{X}$
100,000	$\overline{C}$
500,000	$\overline{D}$
1,000,000	$\overline{M}$

Vocabulary: The Personal Dictionary

K Prefixes

Prefix	General Meaning	Example/s
A		
a(n)-	not, without	amoral, anarchy
acr(o)-	high, up	Acropolis
aer(o)-	air	aeronautics
agr(o)-	to do with farming	agriculture
andr-	man	android
Anglo-	English or British	Anglophone
anthrop(o)-	relating to human beings	anthropology
ant(i)-	against	antidote, antibody
aut(o)-	self	autonomy
B		
bi-	two	bicycle, bilingual
bi(o)-	life	biology
bibli(o)-	relating to books	bibliography
bronch(o)-	relating to breathing	bronchitis
C		
cardi(o)-	heart	cardiovascular
cent-, centi-	hundred or hundredth	centenary, century
chron(o)-	time	chronology
circum-	around	circumference
co-, com-, con-	together, with	cooperative
col-, cor-	together, with	conference
contr(a)-, (o)-	against, opposite	contradiction
counter-	against, opposite	counterpoint
crypt(o)-	hidden	cryptic
D		
de-	take something away, the opposite	dehydration
dec(a)-, dek(a)-	ten	decathlon
deci-	one tenth	decimal
dem(o)-,	people, nation	demographics
derm(o)-, (a)-	skin	dermatology
dynam(o)-	power, force	dynamic
dis-	reverse, opposite	dissent, dislike
dys-	bad, deformed, abnormal	dysfunction
E		
eco-	habitat	economy, ecology
electr(o)-	electricity	electronic
eu-	good	eulogy, eugenics
ex-	former	ex-wife

extra-	very, more than usual, outside, beyond	extraordinary,

F
flor(i)-	relating to flowers	florist, floristry
fore-	before, in advance	foreword

H
hemi-	half	hemisphere
hex(a)-	six	hexagon
hyper-	excessive, *(least to greatest in order: hypo, sub, super, hyper)*	
		hyperactive

I
in-	extremely	inflammable
il-, im-, ir-	not	illiteracy
inter-	between, from one to another	intervention
intra-	within,	interior

K
kilo-	thousand	kilogram

M
mal-	bad, badly	malnutrition
maxi-	most, very, large	maximum
mega-	million, very large	megabyte,
micro-	one millionth, very small	microscopic
mid-	in the middle of	midterm
milli-	thousandth	milligram
mini-	small	minimum
mis-	bad, wrong	misappropriate
mon(o)-	one, single	monopoly
multi-	many	multilingual

N
non-	not, nine	nonsense, none

O
oct(o)-, (a)-	eight	octopus, octagon
over-	more than normal, too much	overpopulation

P
pent(a)-	five	pentagon
post-	after	postmodernism
pre-	before	preview, prepare
pro-	for, in favour of	prochoice, prolife

Vocabulary: The Personal Dictionary

Q
quadr-, quart-	four	quadrangle
quint(i)-	fifth, five	quintuplet

R
re-	again, repeatedly	remember
rect(i)-	proper, straight	rectify, rectangle

S
semi-	half	semidetached
sept(a)-	seven	heptathlon
schiz(o)-, schist(o)-	split	schizophrenia,
sub-	below, less than, under, (least to greatest in order: hypo, sub, super, hyper)	subway, subtitles
super-	extremely, more than, (least to greatest in order: hypo, sub, super, hyper)	supersonic
syn-	along with, together, at the same time	synergy

T
tel(e)-, tel(o)-	far, over a long distance	television
trans-	across, beyond	transfer, *transform*
tri-	three	triangle, tricycle

U
ultra-	extremely, beyond a set limit	ultraviolet
uni-	one, single	unity, uniform

Z
zoo-	relating to animals	zoomorphic, zoology

L Suffixes

Suffix	Meaning	Example/s
-able, -ible	capable of being	edible, presentable
-acy	state or quality	privacy
-al	act or process of, pertaining to	refusal, regional
-ance, -ence	state or quality of	maintenance, eminence, allowance, audience
-ate	become	eradicate
-dom	place/state of being	freedom, kingdom
-en	become	enlighten
-er, -or	one who	trainer, protector
-esque	reminiscent of	picturesque
-ful	notable for	fanciful
-ic, -ical	pertaining to	musical, mythic
-ify, -fy	make or become	terrify
-ious, -ous	characterised by	nutritious, portentous
-ish	having the quality of	fiendish
-ism	doctrine, belief	communism
-ist	one who	chemist
-ity, -ty	quality of	veracity
-ive	having the nature of	creative
-ize, -ise	become	civilise
-less	without	endless
-ment	condition of	argument
-ness	state of being	heaviness
-ship	position held	fellowship
-sion, -tion	state of being	concession, transition
-y	characterised by	sleazy

PART 6

Useful Resources

*Patience, persistence and perspiration
make an unbeatable combination for success.
- Napoleon Hill*

This section provides sample templates that you can use to significantly improve your word power.

- Words that I have learnt (Appendix 1); use it to record your knowledge of new words

- *Personal Learning Objective Sheet* (Appendix 2); use it to write your plan. This template will help you take stock of your progress on a periodic basis.

- *Study Plan* (Appendix 3) is a daily time management template. Use it to plan and view your weekly activities.

- *Personal Reading Record* (Appendix 4); use it to record details of the books you have read.

- *Spelling Practice Sheet* (Appendix 5); use it to practise the spelling of words. It provides the opportunity to spell a word four times.

- *Vocabulary Sheet* (Appendix 6); use it to record new words and their meaning.

- *Word Usage Practice Sheet* (Appendix 7); use it to practise writing sentences with new words.

- *Confusable Words Practice Sheet* (Appendix 8); use it to practise writing sentences with confusable words.

- *Book Review Template* (Appendix 9); use it to record your thoughts on a book you have read.

- *Write Your Own List Of Words* (Appendix 10a and 10b); use each one to write new categories of words.

- *Form Your Own Mnemonics* (Appendix 11); use it to create a mnemonic

Vocabulary: The Personal Dictionary

Appendix 1 Words That I Have Learnt

Tick each box for completion and comprehension (✓)

I can spell and use all the words in this book beginning with the letter:

A ☐
B ☐
C ☐
D ☐
E ☐
F ☐
G ☐
H ☐
I ☐
J ☐
K ☐
L ☐
M ☐
N ☐
O ☐
P ☐
Q ☐
R ☐
S ☐
T ☐
U ☐
V ☐
W ☐
X ☐
Y ☐
Z ☐

Appendix 2 Personal Learning Objective Sheet

Name: _____ **Date:** _____

Objective 1	
Accomplished	**Somewhat Accomplished**	**Not Accomplished**
Comments	
Objective 2	
Accomplished	**Somewhat Accomplished**	**Not Accomplished**
Comments	
Objective 3	
Accomplished	**Somewhat Accomplished**	**Not Accomplished**
Comments	

Vocabulary: The Personal Dictionary

Appendix 3 Study Plan

Time	Mon	Tue	Wed	Thur	Fri	Sat	Sun
5 a.m.							
6 a.m.							
7 a.m.							
8 a.m.							
9 a.m.							
10 a.m.							
11 a.m.							
12 p.m.							
1 p.m.							
2 p.m.							
3 p.m.							
4 p.m.							
5 p.m.							
6 p.m.							
7 p.m.							
8 p.m.							
9 p.m.							
10 p.m.							
11 p.m.							
12 a.m.							
1 a.m.							
2 a.m.							
3 a.m.							
4 a.m.							

Reminder Notes

Appendix 4 Personal Reading Record

Books I will read in the month of:_____20_____

Title   Author
1._____   _____
2._____   _____
3._____   _____
4._____   _____

Books I will read in the month of:_____20_____

Title   Author
1._____   _____
2._____   _____
3._____   _____
4._____   _____

Books I will read in the month of:_____20_____

Title   Author
1._____   _____
2._____   _____
3._____   _____
4._____   _____

Books I will read in the month of:_____20_____

Title   Author
1._____   _____
2._____   _____
3._____   _____
4._____   _____

Vocabulary: The Personal Dictionary

Appendix 5 Spelling Practice Sheet

1st Attempt	2nd Attempt	3rd Attempt	4th Attempt

Appendix 6 Extra Vocabulary Sheet

Word	**Meaning**

Vocabulary: The Personal Dictionary

Appendix 7 Word Usage Practice Sheet

New Word: _____
Sentence:_____
_____

New Word: _____
Sentence:_____
_____

New Word: _____
Sentence:_____
_____

New Word: _____
Sentence:_____
_____

New Word: _____
Sentence:_____
_____

New Word: _____
Sentence:_____
_____

New Word: _____
Sentence:_____
_____

New Word: _____
Sentence:_____
_____

New Word: _____
Sentence:_____
_____

Appendix 8   Confusable Words Practice Sheet

Vocabulary: The Personal Dictionary

Appendix 9 Book Review

Title:_____ Author:_____

Genre:_____ No of Pages:_____
Date:_____20____

Describe the main events of the story:
_____
_____
_____
_____
_____
_____
_____

Did you enjoy reading the book? Yes___   No____
State Why/Why not below:
_____
_____
_____
_____
_____
_____

What new words or expressions have you learnt?
List them below and have a go at writing your own sentences.
_____
_____
_____
_____
_____
_____

Appendix 10A Write Your Own List Of Words

A – Z List of _____

A _____ _____
B _____ _____
C _____ _____
D _____ _____
E _____ _____
F _____ _____
G _____ _____
H _____ _____
I _____ _____
J _____ _____
K _____ _____
L _____ _____
M _____ _____
N _____ _____
O _____ _____
P _____ _____
Q _____ _____
R _____ _____
S _____ _____
T _____ _____
U _____ _____
V _____ _____
W _____ _____
X _____ _____
Y _____ _____
Z _____ _____

Vocabulary: The Personal Dictionary

Appendix 10B

Appendix 11 Mnemonic Form

Mnemonic (Word, Phrase or Sentence):

_____

Letter	Word to help you remember	Word You want to remember

References

King, G. 2000. *Vocabulary Expander (Collins Word Power)*. Collins.

King, G. 2000. *Good Grammar (Collins Word Power)*. Edition. Collins.

Nuga, S. 2008. *Succeed at Psychometric Testing: Practice Tests for Verbal Reasoning Intermediate*. 2nd Edition. Hodder & Stoughton.

Kolln, M. J.;Gray, L.S.; Salvatore, J. (2008).*Understanding English Grammar*. 8th ed. London: Longman. 453.

Aarts, B (2011).*Oxford Modern English Grammar*. Oxford: Oxford University Press. 410.

Greenbaum, S (1996).*The Oxford English Grammar*. Oxford and New York: Oxford University Press. 672.

Nuga, S (2013).*English Grammar and Verbal Reasoning - The Toolkit For Success*. USA: Trafford Publishing. 265.

Blamires, H (2000). *The Penguin Guide To Plain English* . London: Penguin Books Ltd.. 345.

Cambridge Essential English Dictionary, 2011. 2 Edition. Cambridge University Press.

Collins *Dictionary & Thesaurus of the English Language*. 2011. 5th Revised Edition. Collins.

Oxford Dictionaries, 2006. *Concise Oxford English Dictionary*. 11Rev Ed Edition. OUP Oxford.

Oxford Dictionaries, 2013. *Paperback Oxford English Dictionary*. 7 Edition. Oxford University Press

Blamires, H (2000). *The Penguin Guide To Plain English* . London: Penguin Books Ltd.. 345.
Cambridge Essential English Dictionary, 2011. 2 Edition. Cambridge University Press.

Collins *Dictionary & Thesaurus of the English Language*. 2011. 5th Revised Edition. Collins.

Useful Websites

El Camino College. *Direct Learning Activity Verbs - Past Participle.* Available: http://www.elcamino.edu/academics/basicskills/dla_engb_pastparticiple_ecc.pdf. Last accessed 20 Jan 2017.

Useful English. 2016. Useful English: Homonyms Short List. [ONLINE] Available at: http://usefulenglish.ru/writing/homonyms-short-list. [Accessed 28 October 2016].

Easy Pace Learning. 2016. English Grammar Guide. [ONLINE] Available at: http://www.ef.com/english-resources/english-grammar/passive-voice/. [Accessed 28 October 2016].

Web Learn. 2014. Active Voice and Passive Voice in English. [ONLINE] Available at: http://www.weblearn.in/active_passive/. [Accessed 28 October 2016].

College Writing Centre. 2004. Commonly Confused Words. [ONLINE] Available at: http://www.stlcc.edu/Student_Resources/Academic_Resources/Writing_Resources/Grammar_Handouts/commonly_confused_words.pdf. [Accessed 28 October 2016].

FIS. 2016. Using a Dictionary. [ONLINE] Available at: http://esl.fis.edu/learners/advice/dic.htm. [Accessed 28 October 2016].

www.smart-words.org. (2012).*A List of the most commonly used English idioms.* Available: http://www.smart-words.org/quotes-sayings/english-idioms-commonly-used.pdf. Last accessed 20 Jan 2017.

Impulse Corp. (2012).*List of Metaphors.* Available: http://metaphors.com/. Last accessed 20 Jan 2017.

cartiaz.ro.*10000 general knowledge questions and answers*.Available: http://www.keloo.ro/doc/10000_intrebari.pdf. Last accessed 11 Jan 2017.

Linger and Look. (2015).*The Best Oxymoron List.* Available: http://www.lingerandlook.com/Words/Oxymora.htm. Last accessed 15th Feb 2017.

Wikipedia. (2001). Available: https://en.wikipedia.org/wiki/Main_Page. Last accessed 15th Feb 2017.

Love To Know. (2017). *List of Adjective Words.* Available:http://grammar.yourdictionary.com/parts-of-speech/adjectives/list-of-adjective-words.html. Last accessed 2nd Mar 2017.The Persuasion Revolution. (2016).

oxymoronlist.com. (2017). *oxymoron.* Available: http://www.oxymoronlist.com/. Last accessed 2nd Mar 2017.

Literary Devices. (2017). *Literary Devices.* Available: https://literarydevices.net/literary-devices/. Last accessed 2nd Mar 2017.

The Persuasion Revolution. Available: http://www.thepersuasionrevolution.com/380-high-emotion-persuasive-words/. Last accessed 2nd Mar 2017.

TALKENGLISH.com. (2017). *Top 1500 Nouns.* Available: http://www.talkenglish.com/vocabulary/top-1500-nouns.aspx. Last accessed 2nd Mar 2017.

Metaphor List. (2013). *Metaphor List.* Available: http://www.metaphorlist.net/. Last accessed 2nd Mar 2017.

Basic English Grammar. (2017). *Pronouns.* Available: http://www.basic-english-grammar.com/pronouns.html/. Last accessed 2nd Mar 2017.

Oliver, D. (2007). *Idioms: Complete List.* Available: http://www.eslcafe.com/idioms/id-list.html. Last accessed 2nd Mar 2017.

English Grammar Revolution. (2017). *List of Adverbs.* Available: http://www.english-grammar-revolution.com/list-of-adverbs.html. Last accessed 2nd Mar 2017.

Alliterationlist.com. (2013). *Alliteration List.* Available: http://www.alliterationlist.com/. Last accessed 2nd Mar 2017.

World Class Learning. (2017). *List of Countries, Capitals, Currencies, & Languages.* Available: http://www.worldclasslearning.com/general-knowledge/list-countries-capital-currencies-languages.html. Last accessed 2nd Mar 2017.

Crabtree, V. (2013). *A List of All Religions and Belief Systems.* Available: http://www.humanreligions.info/religions.html. Last accessed 11th Mar 2017.

https://en.wikipedia.org. (2017). *RGB color model.* Available: https://en.wikipedia.org/wiki/RGB_color_model. Last accessed 11th Mar 2017.

Kelly, C.; Kelly. L. (2010). *Places In and Around the House.* Available: http://www.manythings.org/vocabulary/lists/a/words.php?f=things_in_a_house. Last accessed 11th Mar 2017.

Published by Liberty Stowe Ltd.
Simbo Nuga PhD, PGCE, MBA, MA, BA (Hons.)
Other books by this author:
Succeed at Psychometric Testing: Practice Tests for Verbal Reasoning (Intermediate). Published by Hodder and Stoughton, 2003.

Succeed at Psychometric Testing: Practice Tests for Verbal Reasoning (Intermediate). Published by Hodder and Stoughton, 2008.

English Grammar and Verbal Reasoning: The Toolkit for Success. Published by Trafford Publishing, 2013.

Practice Tests in Verbal Reasoning: Nearly 3000 Test Exercises with Answers and Explanations. Published by Trafford Publishing, 2013.

Perfect English: The Complete Toolkit. Published by Liberty Stowe, 2017

Vocabulary: Record and Remember. Published by Liberty Stowe, 2017

English Grammar and Verbal Reasoning: The Toolkit for Success. Published by Liberty Stowe Ltd, 2017.

Practice Tests in Verbal Reasoning: Nearly 3000 Test Exercises with Answers and Explanations. Published by Trafford Publishing, 2013.

NOTES

NOTES

NOTES